REVISE BTEC NATIONAL
Computing

REVISION WORKBOOK

Series Consultant: Harry Smith

Authors: Steve Farrell, Mark Fishpool, Christine Gate and Richard McGill

---

A note from the publisher

While the publishers have made every attempt to ensure that advice on the qualificatic
and its assessment is accurate, the official specification and associated assessment
guidance materials are the only authoritative source of information
and should always be referred to for definitive guidance.

This qualification is reviewed on a regular basis and may be updated in the future.
Any such updates that affect the content of this Revision Workbook will be outlined at
www.pearsonfe.co.uk/BTECchanges.

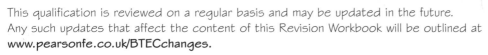

D1076989

**For the full range of Pearson revision titles across KS2,
KS3, GCSE, Functional Skills, AS/A Level and BTEC visit:**
www.pearsonschools.co.uk/revise

Pearson

Published by Pearson Education Limited, 80 Strand, London, WC2R 0RL.

www.pearsonschoolsandfecolleges.co.uk

Copies of official specifications for all Pearson qualifications may be found on the website: qualifications.pearson.com

Text and illustrations © Pearson Education Ltd 2017
Typeset and illustrated by Kamae Design, Oxford
Produced by Out of House Publishing
Cover illustration by Miriam Sturdee

The rights of Richard McGill, Steve Farrell, Christine Gate and Mark Fishpool to be identified as authors of this work has been asserted by them in accordance with the Copyright, Designs and Patents Act 1988.

First published 2017

20 19 18 17
10 9 8 7 6 5 4 3 2 1

British Library Cataloguing in Publication Data
A catalogue record for this book is available from the British Library

ISBN 978 1 292 15019 2

Printed in Slovakia by Neografia

Acknowledgements
All images © Pearson Education

Notes from the publisher

1 While the publishers have made every attempt to ensure that advice on the qualification and its assessment is accurate, the official specification and associated assessment guidance materials are the only authoritative source of information and should always be referred to for definitive guidance.

   Pearson examiners have not contributed to any sections in this resource relevant to examination papers for which they have responsibility.

2 Pearson has robust editorial processes, including answer and fact checks, to ensure the accuracy of the content in this publication, and every effort is made to ensure this publication is free of errors. We are, however, only human, and occasionally errors do occur. Pearson is not liable for any misunderstandings that arise as a result of errors in this publication, but it is our priority to ensure that the content is accurate. If you spot an error, please do contact us at resourcescorrections@pearson.com so we can make sure it is corrected.

Websites
Pearson Education Limited is not responsible for the content of any external internet sites. It is essential for tutors to preview each website before using it in class so as to ensure that the URL is still accurate, relevant and appropriate. We suggest that tutors bookmark useful websites and consider enabling students to access them through the school/ college intranet.

Introduction

This Workbook has been designed to help you revise the skills you may need for the externally assessed units of your course. Remember that you won't necessarily be studying all the units included here – it will depend on the qualification you are taking.

BTEC National Qualification	Externally assessed units
Extended Certificate Foundation Diploma	1 Principles of Computer Science 2 Fundamentals of Computer Systems
Extended Diploma	1 Principles of Computer Science 2 Fundamentals of Computer Systems 3 Planning and Management of Computing Projects 4 Software Design and Development Project

Your Workbook

Each unit in this Workbook contains either one or two sets of revision questions or revision tasks, to help you **revise the skills** you may need in your assessment. The selected content, outcomes, questions and answers used in each unit are provided to help you to revise content and ways of applying your skills. Ask your tutor or check the Pearson website for the most up-to-date **Sample Assessment Material** and **Mark Schemes** to get an indication of the structure of your actual assessment and what this requires of you. The detail of the actual assessment may change so always make sure you are up to date.

Often, you will also find one or more useful features that explain or break down longer questions or tasks. Remember that these features won't appear in your actual assessment!

> Grey boxes like this contain **hints and tips** about ways that you might complete a task, interpret a brief, understand a concept or structure your responses.

 This icon will appear next to an example partial answer to a revision question or revision task. You should read the partial answer carefully, then complete it in your own words.

> This is a **revision activity**. It will help you understand the processes or steps you could take in completing a revision question or task.

>  These boxes will tell you where you can find more help in Pearson's BTEC National Revision Guide.
Visit **www.pearsonschools.co.uk/revise** for more information.

There is often space on the pages for you to write in. However, if you are carrying out research and making ongoing notes, you may want to use separate paper. Similarly, some units will be assessed through submission of digital files, or on screen, rather than on paper. Ask your tutor or check the Pearson website for the most up-to-date Sample Assessment Material to get an idea of the structure of the assessed exams or tasks and what is required of you.

Contents

Revision Guide also available for externally assessed units ISBN 9781292150208

Unit 1: Principles of Computer Science

	1	Your exam
Guided	2	Revision test 1
	22	Revision test 2

Unit 2: Fundamentals of Computer Systems

	37	Your exam
Guided	38	Revision test 1
	51	Revision test 2

Unit 3: Planning and Management of Computing Projects

	64	Your set task
Guided	65	Revision task 1
	88	Revision task 2

Unit 4: Software Design and Development Project

	107	Your set task
Guided	108	Revision task 1
	133	Revision task 2

138	Answers

A small bit of small print

Pearson publishes Sample Assessment Material and the Specification on its website. This is the official content and this book should be used in conjunction with it. The questions in this book have been written to help you practise the knowledge and skills you will require for your assessment. Remember: the real assessment may not look like this.

Unit 1:
Principles of Computer Science

Your exam

Unit 1 will be assessed through an exam, which will be set by Pearson. You will need to use your computational thinking skills to solve computing problems through your response to questions that require short and long answers.

Your Revision Workbook

> This workbook is designed to **revise skills** that might be needed in your exam. The selected content, outcomes, questions and answers are provided to help you to revise content and ways of applying your skills. Ask your tutor or check the **Pearson website** for the most up-to-date **Sample Assessment Material** and **Mark Scheme** to get an indication of the structure of your actual exam and what this requires of you. The details of the actual exam may change so always make sure you are up to date.

To support your revision, this workbook contains revision questions to help you revise the skills that might be needed in your exam.

Your response to the questions will help you to revise:

- computational thinking
- standard methods and techniques used to develop algorithms
- programming paradigms
- types of programming and markup languages.

> **Links** To help you revise skills that might be needed in your Unit 1 exam, this workbook contains two sets of revision questions starting on pages 2 and 22. The first is guided and models good techniques, to help you develop your skills. The second gives you the opportunity to apply the skills you have developed. See the introduction on page iii for more information on features included to help you revise.

Revision test 1

To support your revision, the questions below help you to revise the skills that you might need in your exam. The revision test is divided into four questions, each based on a different scenario. You will need to refer to the information sheets on pages 14–21 in order to answer some of the questions. The details of the actual exam may change, so always make sure you are up-to-date. Ask your tutor or check the Pearson website for the most up-to-date Sample Assessment Material to get an idea of the structure of your exam and what this requires of you.

 Links Please refer to Sections 1 and 2 of the information sheets on pages 14–16 in order to answer Revision Question 1.

Guided **1** Tanya is creating a 2D computer game. The user drives a taxi around the screen. Success is measured by how much money has been earned and how few penalty points have been added to the driving licence. Variables are used to hold both of these quantities.

A design for the Level 1 screen and the Level 1 design criteria are given in Section 1 of the information sheets on page 14.

Driving licence points will be given as variables.

(a) Identify **three** features of the game proposal, other than driving licence points, that would be represented as a variable.

3 marks

1 Taxi sprite X coordinate

2 ....

3 ....

> The variables will be anything inside the program where the value changes as the game runs.

During part of the play the user picks up passengers at £25, £20, £15, £12, £28 and £13, and has a driving fine of £50. The amount of money at the start of this play was £65.

(b) Calculate how much money was available at the end of this play.
You are advised to show your working.

2 marks

Start of play money + (passenger fares) – driving fine =

£65 +

> You will need to show your workings for the calculations you made in reaching your answer.

(c) Produce pseudocode that describes the movement of Taxi sprite when the user presses the right arrow key.

4 marks

Your pseudocode needs to include keywords (in UPPER case) and to carefully sequence the actions. Use an indent for the actions following a **structure keyword** such as IF. (Don't forget to remove it for the next structure keyword).

Guided
```
BEGIN
IF key held down
   Increase speed
```

....

....

....

....

....

....

....

....

....

> **Links** You can find more information on producing pseudocode in the Revision Guide, pages 9, 10 and 141.

Tanya writes some code to handle the keyboard inputs needed to move the Taxi sprite, which is shown in Section 2 of the information sheets on page 15.

(d) Identify **two** examples of duplicated code in this program section which responds to the Ctrl key. How can these duplicate codes be simplified?

4 marks

Example 1

Code responding to the Ctrl key is duplicated in lines 6–14, 18–26, 30–38, 42–50. This code is only needed once at the start of the subroutine.

> You will need to follow the code carefully to be able to answer this revision question. Look for duplicated code that can be reduced.

Example 2

....

....

....

(e) Identify **two** examples of poor code in this section of programming, which mean the program is unlikely to work as intended. Explain how to improve the effectiveness of this code.

4 marks

1 The duplicated code responding to the Ctrl key in lines 6–14, 18–26, 30–38, 42–50, is flawed as it cannot reduce MoveDistance. The code needs to respond to

> Follow all the conditional statements (IF) to ensure that they will all work as intended.

....

2 ....

....

....

....

Programmers can use flow charts to plan the logic for their programs. Tanya has produced a flow chart (Figure 3 on page 16) to show the logic for:

- actions when the Ctrl key is pressed
- checking when a movement would collide the Taxi sprite with a wall
- responding to entry into a square (this should be shown as a process box in this flow chart, with no need to include the detailed logic).

(f) Identify an example of each of the following in the flow chart, by writing text from a flow chart symbol into your answer.

4 marks

Decision

Ctrl key pressed?

Input/output

> You will need to identify the correct symbol, then carefully copy the words in the box into your answers.

....

Process

....

Start/end

....

(g) State the conventions for using the flow arrows in a flow chart.

2 marks

The default directions of flow are to the right or downwards.

Each flow line should have an arrowhead at one end which

> Flow lines connect the symbols together in a flow chart.

....

....

....

Links There are two important aspects of producing a flow chart. It needs to use the standard BCS flow chart symbols and to accurately represent the flows (pathways) that are possible through a program. The flows should default as down or right, with arrows to confirm the direction to follow. Be careful to show the decision questions and to label the routes out of them (for example YES and NO). You can find more on how to produce a flow chart on pages 11 and 140 of the Revision Guide.

Total for Revision Question 1 = 23 marks

Links Please refer to Section 3 on page 17 in order to answer Revision Question 2.

Guided 2 Aarav runs dance classes. He is creating a program to administer the start every three months, with three sessions a week at different locations on different days. Standard membership entitles a customer to attend 12 sessions on days of their choice during the three months.

Part of the programming code is given on page 17.

The programming code Aarav created contains at least one bug, so he decides to use input boxes for rapid data entry to test the outcomes.

(a) Give the expected outputs from lblMemberFee. Find the text for these data entries (with the actual outcomes the code would produce) by completing the table. **3 marks**

First input	Second input	Expected output	Actual output
n	S	35	35
y	S	28	
N	M	50	50
Y	M	40	
N	p	75	
Y	p	60	

Program code is very precise and will only do the exact actions written. Be careful with individual characters: upper and lower case versions are treated as different.

You will need to fill in all the blank boxes in the 'Expected output' and 'Actual output' columns in the table.

(b) Name the control structures used in Aarav's code with their key words. **2 marks**

Loop (UNTIL)

The other structure will be a branch.

....

(c) Describe how a programmer can avoid input errors from capitalisation, for example, if the user types in 'n' rather than an expected 'N'. **3 marks**

Capitalisation becomes important for short inputs such as single characters or acronyms which are used in comparisons by code. If a text box is used

for input ....

The programmer has a choice of whether to use a control that has a defined output, such as a checkbox, or to allow the user to type in a response, which will require code to allow for variations such as upper/lower case.

....

....

....

....

Attendance at sessions for each student are kept in a two-dimensional array called 'Bookings'.

(d)   Explain why this is an appropriate data structure for this application.

4 marks

The two dimensions of an array called 'Bookings' will provide an appropriate data structure for holding the attendances of members for the dancing sessions. One dimension, the rows, can be used for the members, and the other dimension, the columns, can be used for the sessions.

> Your answer should be well structured and clear on the points you make. There are four marks for this revision question so you should include at least four points in your response.

....

....

....

....

....

....

 Links The array is a data structure widely used in code as a variable containing several data items. For information on arrays, see the Revision Guide, page 23.

The program needs to sort the member attendance for a session into ascending order.

(e)   Demonstrate how a bubble sort can be used to sort the data in the 'Before' row for the first dancing session by completing the table.

4 marks

	Array(1)	Array(2)	Array(3)	Array(4)	Array(5)	Array(6)
Before	NJI	GM2	REI	JM2	JB3	GMI
	GM2	NJI	REI	JM2	JB3	GMI
	GM2	NJI	JM2	REI	JB3	GMI
					REI	
						REI
			NJI			
	GM2	JM2	JB3	NJI	GMI	REI
	GM2	JB3	JM2	GMI	NJI	REI
	GM2	JB3	GMI	JM2	NJI	REI
After	GMI	GM2	JB3	JM2	NJI	REI

> Complete the blank boxes in the Array(1)–Array(6) columns.

 Links Revise how a bubble sort works on page 26 of the Revision Guide.

Aarav's programming code (see page 17) uses variables for testing the logic.

(f)   Identify **two** variables in the code that could be declared as global variables and explain why this would be an appropriate scope structure for them.   3 marks

1   MemberFee could be suitable for declaring as a global variable. This would be an appropriate scope for this variable because the fee will be different for another member and the contents of this variable could be useful in other parts of the code.

> You need to identify two variables which hold values that can be used in other parts of the program. Variable 1 above identifies MemberFee. There are another two potential global variables in the code given in the information pages on page 17.
>
> You could start by identifying which of these variables would be better declared as constants.

2   ....

    ....

> **Links**   A global variable exists everywhere in the code and only ceases when the app closes. To revise global variables, see the Revision Guide, pages 14 and 154.

Aarav's programming code could use some global constants, rather than variables.

(g)   State why a programmer would choose to use a **constant** in preference to a **variable**.   3 marks

A constant is very similar to a variable except that the data it holds does not normally change as the program runs.

> Start by identifying the main difference between variables and constants.

....

....

....

....

Total for Revision Question 2 = 22 marks

Guided 3 A chef working in a gastropub writes a program to help her keep track of the recipes used in the kitchen. Each recipe has a type which may be a page-referenced in a cookery book, cut-out from a magazine, link to a web page, a hand-written note or printout.

When a new recipe is entered, the system allocates a reference based upon the type.

The chef has written some pseudocode to show the logic for how this reference is made (with comments at the end of some lines after single quotes).

```
BEGIN
INPUT Type                          'From a combo box

IF Type = "page reference"
    Ref = "PR"                      'page reference
ELSE
    Ref = "CO"                      'cut-out from a magazine
IF Type = "link to a web page"
    Ref = "WP"                      'link to a web page
IF Type = "hand-written notes"
    Ref ="HW"                       'hand-written notes
Ref = Random()                      'Add a random number to the reference
END
```

(a) Identify **two** errors in this pseudocode, and how each of the errors could be fixed.   4 marks

1 ELSE statement will not reliably respond to 'cut-out from a magazine' selected from the combo box.
   Replace ELSE statement with IF Type = "cut-out"

> The ELSE statement will wrongly identify all selections from the combo box, other than "page reference", as "cut-out from a magazine".
>
> Identify another error and explain how to fix it.

2 ....

....

....

....

The program allocates a unique reference to each item, such as HW032 for a hand-written recipe, where the first two characters indicate the type.

(b) Explain **two** ways an item's reference can be used when the program runs.   4 marks

1 The first two letters of the reference can be used to sort items by type.

> Answer (1) explains how the first part of the reference can be used by the program to sequence an array or other structure to separate out the types of reference.
>
> How else could the first two letters of the reference be used by the program from user input?

2 ....

....

....

....

....

The chef decides to add a text box where the first two letters of a reference can be typed to search for that type of recipe.

(c) State **two** validation rules that could be applied to this text box.

Rule

"CO" OR "HW" OR "PO" OR "PR" OR "WP"

> You need to explain why this would be effective in preventing bad data from being entered.

Reason

....

(d) Discuss how single- or multi-dimensional arrays could be used to keep track of recipes for the chef.

Single-dimensional arrays are a poor choice for this usage as at least three arrays would be needed to hold the reference number, description and where the recipe is located. Synchronising these into the same order would be a little more difficult than multi-dimensional arrays, especially if sorting needs to be coded into the program.

Multi-dimensional arrays are a good option, with a choice of ....

> Your answer could start with a summary to confirm why you think arrays are an appropriate data structure for code to meet this problem.

....

....

....

....

....

....

....

....

> **Links** A one-dimensional array has a single subscript inside the brackets and can be thought of as a single list of items. A multi-dimensional array has two (or more) subscripts inside the brackets and can be thought of as being able to hold a table of data. To revise arrays, see the Revision Guide, page 23.

The program used to keep track of recipes for the chef needs to be able to save the data to backup storage before it is closed and to retrieve this information when opened.

(e) Analyse how the program code will output the recipes' information to one or more data files and how code could input this data back into the program.

6 marks

Program code needs to be able to output the recipes information to data file(s), otherwise any data in the arrays will be lost when the program closes. Similarly, this data needs to be input back into the program when it starts.

> Continue the answer by analysing the types of loops that are most appropriate, using FOR to output the data, as the number of items are known, and any of the other loop types for input so they can continue iterating until the end of the data file.

Code to both output and input data will use loops to go through data ....

....

....

....

....

....

....

....

....

....

....

Total for Revision Question 3 = 22 marks

Links Please refer to Sections 4 and 5 of the information sheets on pages 18–21 in order to answer Revision Question 4.

Guided 4 Richard is creating a program to help him practise scales on a bass guitar.

A design for the screen and the design criteria are given in Section 4 of the information sheets on page 18. Code written to implement the program is shown in Section 5 on pages 19–21.

Program code uses structures to control program flow and to hold data.

(a) Name the variable types defined in these lines of code. **2 marks**

Line 4: Integer variable

Line 8: ....

> Make sure you look at the correct line numbers and include as much as you can about the variable defined on each of these lines of code.

(b) Draw a flow chart to represent lines 149 to 151 of Richard's code. **3 marks**

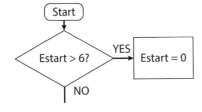

> Be careful to represent which actions are dependent on the IF statement.

(c) Discuss any features of object orientated programming that could be used to code Richard's problem.

6 marks

> Your answer should start with an overview of the features that are identified, followed by expansions of how each of these features could be utilised in the program code.

Object-orientated programming could be used to code Richard's problem using abstraction, inheritance and initial design for the program around real objects.

The program could be designed using an object-orientated approach, for example, the scales and fretboard being separate objects.

....

....

....

The first display could use abstraction to ....

....

....

....

Inheritance can be used to ....

....

....

....

(d) Evaluate the code Richard has written and produce suggestions on how this code can be improved.

12 marks

The code Richard has written can be improved in several ways.

Objects should be given meaningful names. The code has a button named Button1, which does not help this or future programmers ....

....

....

> Look for other examples of poor coding and describe what you would do to rectify the problem.

The code should respond to ....

....

....

....

....

....

The code starting "G string" ....

....

....

....

....

....

....

....

....

....

....

....

....

....

....

....

....

....

....

....

....

....

Describe examples of any good practice you find.

Despite these issues, there are some examples of good practice.

....

....

....

....

Total for Revision Question 4 = 23 marks

END OF REVISION TEST 1

TOTAL FOR REVISION TEST 1 = 90 MARKS

Information for Revision test 1

The information below should be used to answer some of the revision questions on pages 2–13. The information is divided into five sections, with each section relating to a specific revision question. The details of the actual exam may change, so always make sure you are up to date. Ask your tutor or check the Pearson website for the most up-to-date Sample Assessment Material to get an idea of the structure of your exam and what this requires of you.

SECTION 1

Links The information in this section should be used to answer Revision Question 1(a) on page 2.

Figure 1 shows a design for the Level 1 screen from the game that Tanya has created.

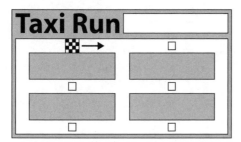

Figure 1

A sprite representing a taxi will start on the chequered grid.

The screen for Level 1 of the game must meet the following design criteria.

- The taxi sprite will:
  - not be able to enter or cross any of the grey areas
  - keep moving in an XY direction set by the arrow keys
  - be accelerated or slowed by holding down an arrow key. The sprite moves 2, 4 or 6 units, matching the time the key has been held down.
- The white squares will:
  - change every second to become white, black or not visible
  - show white when they offer a positive outcome such as picking up a passenger
  - show black when they offer a negative outcome such as a speeding fine
  - have no impact when they are not visible.
- Progress will be tracked by:
  - money, which is:
    - increased by a new passenger
    - reduced by insurance, car tax, motoring fines
  - driving licence points, which are:
    - increased by motoring fines
    - reduced by a driving ban.

SECTION 2

 Links The information in this section should be used to answer Revision Question 1(d) on page 3.

Figure 2 shows the code that Tanya first wrote to respond to key presses and to move the Taxi sprite.

```
1  ⊟Public Class Form1
2        Dim MoveDistance = 2
3
4  ⊟      Private Sub Form1_KeyDown(sender As Object, e As System.Windows.Forms.KeyEventArgs) Handles Me.KeyDown
5            If e.KeyCode = 37 Then   'Left arrow pressed
6                If Control.ModifierKeys = Keys.Control Then
7                    If MoveDistance = -6 Then MoveDistance = -6
8                    If MoveDistance = -4 Then MoveDistance = -6
9                    If MoveDistance = -2 Then MoveDistance = -4
10                   If MoveDistance = 0 Then MoveDistance = -2
11                   If MoveDistance = 2 Then MoveDistance = 0
12                   If MoveDistance = 4 Then MoveDistance = 2
13                   If MoveDistance = 6 Then MoveDistance = 4
14               End If
15               sprTaxi.Top = sprTaxi.Top - MoveDistance
16           End If
17           If e.KeyCode = 38 Then   'Up arrow pressed
18               If Control.ModifierKeys = Keys.Control Then
19                   If MoveDistance = -6 Then MoveDistance = -6
20                   If MoveDistance = -4 Then MoveDistance = -6
21                   If MoveDistance = -2 Then MoveDistance = -4
22                   If MoveDistance = 0 Then MoveDistance = -2
23                   If MoveDistance = 2 Then MoveDistance = 0
24                   If MoveDistance = 4 Then MoveDistance = 2
25                   If MoveDistance = 6 Then MoveDistance = 4
26               End If
27               sprTaxi.Left = sprTaxi.Left + MoveDistance
28           End If
29           If e.KeyCode = 39 Then   'Right arrow pressed
30               If Control.ModifierKeys = Keys.Control Then
31                   If MoveDistance = -6 Then MoveDistance = -4
32                   If MoveDistance = -4 Then MoveDistance = -2
33                   If MoveDistance = -2 Then MoveDistance = 0
34                   If MoveDistance = 0 Then MoveDistance = 2
35                   If MoveDistance = 2 Then MoveDistance = 4
36                   If MoveDistance = 4 Then MoveDistance = 6
37                   If MoveDistance = 6 Then MoveDistance = 6
38               End If
39               sprTaxi.Left = sprTaxi.Left + MoveDistance
40           End If
41           If e.KeyCode = 40 Then   'Down arrow pressed
42               If Control.ModifierKeys = Keys.Control Then
43                   If MoveDistance = -6 Then MoveDistance = -4
44                   If MoveDistance = -4 Then MoveDistance = -2
45                   If MoveDistance = -2 Then MoveDistance = 0
46                   If MoveDistance = 0 Then MoveDistance = 2
47                   If MoveDistance = 2 Then MoveDistance = 4
48                   If MoveDistance = 4 Then MoveDistance = 6
49                   If MoveDistance = 6 Then MoveDistance = 6
50               End If
51               sprTaxi.Top = sprTaxi.Top + MoveDistance
52           End If
```

Figure 2

Figure 3 shows the flow chart that Tanya drew to help plan writing the code to move the Taxi sprite.

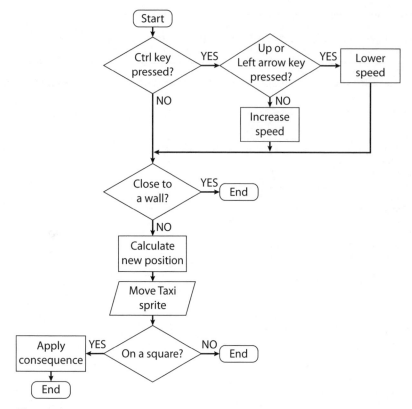

Figure 3

SECTION 3

🔗 **Links** The information in this section should be used to answer Revision Question 2(a) on page 5.

Figure 4 shows the code that Aarav wrote to help debug calculating membership fees.

```
Public Class Form1

    Private Sub btnTester_Click(sender As System.Object, e As System.EventArgs) Handles btnTester.Click

        Dim MemberFee, PreviousDiscount, RatePremium, RateProfessional, RateStandard As Single
        Dim MemberType, PreviousMember As Char
        Do Until (MemberType = "Q")
            MemberFee = 0
            PreviousDiscount = 0.8
            RateStandard = 35
            RatePremium = 50
            RateProfessional = 75
            PreviousMember = InputBox("Enter if a previous member")
            MemberType = InputBox("Enter member type" & vbCrLf & "(S=standard M=premium P=professional)")
            If PreviousMember = "Y" Then MemberFee = MemberFee * PreviousDiscount
            If MemberType = "S" Then MemberFee = RateStandard
            If MemberType = "M" Then MemberFee = RatePremium
            If MemberType = "P" Then MemberFee = RateProfessional
            lblMemberFee.Text = MemberFee
        Loop
    End Sub
End Class
```

Figure 4

SECTION 4

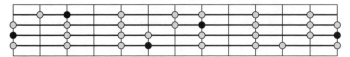

Links The information in this section should be used to answer Revision Question 4(a) on page 11.

Part of learning to play a musical instrument may involve practising scales – a set of musical notes played in sequence going up or down. Every scale has a root note where it starts, shown as black dots in Figure 5 below for a bass guitar. The scale notes are always the same distance apart.

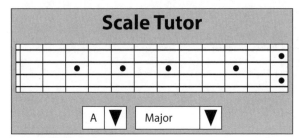

Figure 5

Richard is writing a Windows app to show where a scale can be played on the fretboard of a bass guitar. Figure 6 shows the screen design he has produced:

Scale Tutor

Figure 6

Combo boxes are to be used to select the key (e.g. A) and the scale (e.g. Major). Once selected, the positions on the bass fretboard where the scale is played are to be identified using labels which the code positions into the correct places. Figure 6 shows the positions for the scale of A Major.

SECTION 5

 Links The information in this section should be used to answer Revision Question 4(b) on page 11.

Figure 7 shows the code that Richard first wrote to produce his program. It is written using VB.NET.

```
Public Class Form1
    Private Sub Button1_Click(sender As System.Object, e As System.EventArgs) Handles Button1.Click
        Dim GstringY = 65, DstringY = 110, AstringY = 155, EstringY = 200
        Dim I, Gstart, Dstart, Astart, Estart As Integer
        Dim CurrentG, CurrentD, CurrentA, CurrentE As Integer
        Static BeenThere = False

        Dim Scales(5, 6) As Integer
        Scales(0, 0) = 2
        Scales(0, 1) = 2
        Scales(0, 2) = 1
        Scales(0, 3) = 2
        Scales(0, 4) = 2
        Scales(0, 5) = 2
        Scales(0, 6) = 1

        Dim Xpos() As Integer = {20, 120, 220, 320, 420}
        Dim subsets() As Control = {lblN1, lblN2, lblN3, lblN4, lblN5, lblN6, lblN7, lblN8,
        Dim Amajor As New List(Of Point)

        'G string
        Gstart = 5
        CurrentG = 84
        Amajor.Add(New Point(CurrentG, GstringY))
        Gstart = Gstart + 1
        If Gstart > 6 Then Gstart = 0
        CurrentG = CurrentG + Scales(0, Gstart) * 84
        Amajor.Add(New Point(CurrentG, GstringY))
        Gstart = Gstart + 1
        If Gstart > 6 Then Gstart = 0
        CurrentG = CurrentG + Scales(0, Gstart) * 84
        Amajor.Add(New Point(CurrentG, GstringY))
        Gstart = Gstart + 1
        If Gstart > 6 Then Gstart = 0
        CurrentG = CurrentG + Scales(0, Gstart) * 84
        Amajor.Add(New Point(CurrentG, GstringY))
        Gstart = Gstart + 1
        If Gstart > 6 Then Gstart = 0
        CurrentG = CurrentG + Scales(0, Gstart) * 84
        Amajor.Add(New Point(CurrentG, GstringY))
        Gstart = Gstart + 1
        If Gstart > 6 Then Gstart = 0
        CurrentG = CurrentG + Scales(0, Gstart) * 84
        Amajor.Add(New Point(CurrentG, GstringY))
        Gstart = Gstart + 1
        If Gstart > 6 Then Gstart = 0
        CurrentG = CurrentG + Scales(0, Gstart) * 84
        Amajor.Add(New Point(CurrentG, GstringY))
        Gstart = Gstart + 1
        If Gstart > 6 Then Gstart = 0
        CurrentG = CurrentG + Scales(0, Gstart) * 84
        Amajor.Add(New Point(CurrentG, GstringY))

        'D string
        Dstart = 2
        CurrentD = 0
        Amajor.Add(New Point(CurrentD, DstringY))
        Dstart = Dstart + 1
        If Dstart > 6 Then Dstart = 0
        CurrentD = CurrentD + Scales(0, Dstart) * 84
        Amajor.Add(New Point(CurrentD, DstringY))
        Dstart = Dstart + 1
        If Dstart > 6 Then Dstart = 0
        CurrentD = CurrentD + Scales(0, Dstart) * 84
        Amajor.Add(New Point(CurrentD, DstringY))
        Dstart = Dstart + 1
        If Dstart > 6 Then Dstart = 0
        CurrentD = CurrentD + Scales(0, Dstart) * 84
```

```
Amajor.Add(New Point(CurrentD, DstringY))
Dstart = Dstart + 1
If Dstart > 6 Then Dstart = 0
CurrentD = CurrentD + Scales(0, Dstart) * 84
Amajor.Add(New Point(CurrentD, DstringY))
Dstart = Dstart + 1
If Dstart > 6 Then Dstart = 0
CurrentD = CurrentD + Scales(0, Dstart) * 84
Amajor.Add(New Point(CurrentD, DstringY))
Dstart = Dstart + 1
If Dstart > 6 Then Dstart = 0
CurrentD = CurrentD + Scales(0, Dstart) * 84
Amajor.Add(New Point(CurrentD, DstringY))
Dstart = Dstart + 1
If Dstart > 6 Then Dstart = 0
CurrentD = CurrentD + Scales(0, Dstart) * 84
Amajor.Add(New Point(CurrentD, DstringY))

'A string
Astart = 6
CurrentA = 0
Amajor.Add(New Point(CurrentA, AstringY))
Astart = Astart + 1
If Astart > 6 Then Astart = 0
CurrentA = CurrentA + Scales(0, Astart) * 84
Amajor.Add(New Point(CurrentA, AstringY))
Astart = Astart + 1
If Astart > 6 Then Astart = 0
CurrentA = CurrentA + Scales(0, Astart) * 84
Amajor.Add(New Point(CurrentA, AstringY))
Astart = Astart + 1
If Astart > 6 Then Astart = 0
CurrentA = CurrentA + Scales(0, Astart) * 84
Amajor.Add(New Point(CurrentA, AstringY))
Astart = Astart + 1
If Astart > 6 Then Astart = 0
CurrentA = CurrentA + Scales(0, Astart) * 84
Amajor.Add(New Point(CurrentA, AstringY))
Astart = Astart + 1
If Astart > 6 Then Astart = 0
CurrentA = CurrentA + Scales(0, Astart) * 84
Amajor.Add(New Point(CurrentA, AstringY))
Astart = Astart + 1
If Astart > 6 Then Astart = 0
CurrentA = CurrentA + Scales(0, Astart) * 84
Amajor.Add(New Point(CurrentA, AstringY))

'E string
Estart = 3
CurrentE = 0
Amajor.Add(New Point(CurrentE, EstringY))
Estart = Estart + 1
If Estart > 6 Then Estart = 0
CurrentE = CurrentE + Scales(0, Estart) * 84
Amajor.Add(New Point(CurrentE, EstringY))
Estart = Estart + 1
If Estart > 6 Then Estart = 0
CurrentE = CurrentE + Scales(0, Estart) * 84
Amajor.Add(New Point(CurrentE, EstringY))
Estart = Estart + 1
If Estart > 6 Then Estart = 0
CurrentE = CurrentE + Scales(0, Estart) * 84
Amajor.Add(New Point(CurrentE, EstringY))
Estart = Estart + 1
If Estart > 6 Then Estart = 0
CurrentE = CurrentE + Scales(0, Estart) * 84
Amajor.Add(New Point(CurrentE, EstringY))
Estart = Estart + 1
If Estart > 6 Then Estart = 0
CurrentE = CurrentE + Scales(0, Estart) * 84
Amajor.Add(New Point(CurrentE, EstringY))
Estart = Estart + 1
```

```vbnet
        If Estart > 6 Then Estart = 0
        CurrentE = CurrentE + Scales(0, Estart) * 84
        Amajor.Add(New Point(CurrentE, EstringY))
        Estart = Estart + 1
        If Estart > 6 Then Estart = 0
        CurrentE = CurrentE + Scales(0, Estart) * 84
        Amajor.Add(New Point(CurrentE, EstringY))

        If Not BeenThere Then
            Amajor.Clear()
            BeenThere = True
            For Each s In subsets
                s.Visible = False
            Next
        Else
            BeenThere = False
        End If

        i = 0
        For Each p As Point In Amajor
            subsets(i).Location = p
            subsets(i).Visible = True
            i = i + 1
        Next

    End Sub

    Private Sub Button2_Click(sender As System.Object, e As System.EventArgs) Handles Button2.Click
        lblN10.Location = New System.Drawing.Point(400, 159)
    End Sub

    Private Sub Form1_Load(sender As System.Object, e As System.EventArgs) Handles MyBase.Load
        ComboBox1.Items.Add("A")
        ComboBox1.Items.Add("A#")
        ComboBox1.Items.Add("B")
        ComboBox1.Items.Add("C")
        ComboBox1.Items.Add("C#")
        ComboBox1.Items.Add("D")
        ComboBox1.Items.Add("D#")
        ComboBox1.Items.Add("E")
        ComboBox1.Items.Add("F")
        ComboBox1.Items.Add("F#")
        ComboBox1.Items.Add("G")
        ComboBox1.Items.Add("G#")

        ComboBox2.Items.Add("Dorian")
        ComboBox2.Items.Add("Harmonic minor")
        ComboBox2.Items.Add("Major")
        ComboBox2.Items.Add("Melodic minor")
        ComboBox2.Items.Add("Natural minor")
        ComboBox2.Items.Add("Pentatonic")

    End Sub
End Class
```

Figure 7

Revision test 2

The questions below help you to revise the skills that you might need in your exam. The revision test is divided into four questions, each based on a different scenario. You will need to refer to pages 34–36 in order to answer some of the questions. The details of the actual exam may change, so always make sure you are up to date. Ask your tutor or check the Pearson website for the most up-to-date Sample Assessment Material to get an idea of the structure of your exam and what this requires of you.

 Links Please refer to Section 1 of the information sheets on page 34 in order to answer Revision Question 1.

1 Vanessa is creating a game named Numb Brrr!

A design for the Level 1 screen and the Level 1 design criteria are given in Section 1 of the information sheets on page 34.

(a) Describe **two** key processes that will be needed by this game.   2 marks

Your answer must include brief descriptions of two key processes.

1 ....

....

2 ....

....

(b) Produce an algorithm using pseudocode to respond to the user input of an answer.   3 marks

You will need to respond to both correct and incorrect user answers.

Remember to use indentation to show actions from the IF and ELSE branches.

....

....

....

....

....

....

....

....

....

....

(c) Describe ways that date/time, floating point (real) and integer variables can be used in the program.   `3 marks`

> Include an example for each data type.

Date/time: ....

....

Floating point (real): ....

....

Integer: ....

....

(d) Explain how alphanumeric string, string, Boolean and character variable data types are best used.   `4 marks`

> Include a use for each data type.

Alphanumeric string: ....

....

String: ....

....

Boolean: ....

....

Character: ....

....

Vanessa encounters an 'Out of range' error message when testing her code.

(e) Describe what might cause this error to occur.   `3 marks`

> Define subscripts and then describe these errors.

....

....

....

....

....

....

(f)   Explain how this app can use previous performances from the user to identify patterns and so produce targeted questions in a current set of exercises.

3 marks

Try to identify three patterns that can be used.

....

....

....

....

....

....

....

....

....

....

Total for Revision Question 1 = 18 marks

Links Please refer to Section 2 of the information sheets on page 35 in order to answer Revision Question 2.

2 A bed and breakfast business is developing a computerised booking system.

Computational thinking involves pattern generalisation and abstraction.

(a) Explain **four** general terms used to represent parts of a problem or system. `4 marks`

Identify and describe each of the four general terms.

1 ....

....

2 ....

....

3 ....

....

4 ....

....

(b) Explain how a function and a subroutine are used in program code. `4 marks`

Remember to define a function and a subroutine, clearly identifying the main difference between them.

1 ....

....

....

....

....

2 ....

....

....

....

....

A function is to return a discount code based upon previous stays at the hotel.
Discount rates of A, B or C are available to guests for new bookings.

Rate A is available if one of the following conditions is met:
- LastOrderDate within last 60 days
- SalesInYear equal to or more than SalesTarget
- OrderValue more than the ExtrasAmount

Rate B is available if any two of the conditions are met.

Rate C is available if all of the conditions are met.

(c) Develop a function definition as pseudocode to accept parameters of LastOrderDate, SalesInYear, OrderValue. The function should return a discount rate of A, B or C. **4 marks**

> Make sure you include the function name and its parameters. Discount rate should be set to null near start of function, correct logic to set discount rates and the return value defined.

....

....

....

....

....

....

....

....

....

....

....

....

....

(d) Describe how global variables can be used in any program. **3 marks**

> You will need to define global variables before explaining how they can be used.

....

....

....

....

....

....

....

(e) Explain how a While control structure can be used for validation of user input.

3 marks

Describe how code inside this loop can validate the inputs.

....

....

....

....

....

....

....

....

(f) Identify range checks validated in the pseudocode by ticking each box in the table which shows a valid data entry.

The pseudocode can be seen in Section 2 of the information sheets on page 35.

3 marks

You need to follow the pseudocode carefully in order to identify the validation of each row in this table.

	000–199	200–399	400–599	600–799	800–999
AAD					
CSD					
GTH					
WWS					

(g) Draw a flow chart to represent the pseudocode shown in Section 2 of the information sheets on page 35.

4 marks

Use BCS flow chart symbols and try to reproduce the pseudocode logic exactly.

Total for Revision Question 2 = 25 marks

3 A test track is setting up a computerised system to keep records of people who book time on the track with their vehicles. Each lap time will be recorded into this system.

(a) Describe why decomposition is needed when designing a programmed solution to this problem.

Include how decomposition helps understanding and communication.

....

....

....

....

....

....

....

(b) Explain why records are a more appropriate data structure than an array to hold information about the customers.

3 marks

Your answer should focus on the need to hold different data types – remember to include examples.

....

....

....

....

....

....

....

(c) Produce a quick sort using these track lap times by completing the table. Use the last item in Array(6) as the pivot.

6 marks

	Array(1)	Array(2)	Array (3)	Array(4)	Array(5)	Array(6)
Before	35	12	36	27	20	4
After	4	12	20	27	35	36

Your answer should fit into the rows provided.

It has been suggested that a bubble sort will work just as well as a quick sort and be much easier to understand.

(d) Analyse the bubble sort over the quick sort algorithm.

8 marks

Your answer should be clear on the best uses of these sort algorithms.

....

....

....

....

....

....

....

....

....

....

....

....

....

....

....

....

....

....

....

....

....

....

....

....

....

....

Total for Revision Question 3 = 20 marks

Links Please refer to Section 3 of the information sheets on page 36 in order to answer Revision Question 4.

4 Kerri makes celebration cakes which she sells directly to customers through her website. She is creating a program to keep track of the cakes she produces.

(a) Demonstrate how a binary search would work for finding item 4200 in a data set ordered from 1 to 8192. Calculate the points where the data is divided to implement this search. `6 marks`

Be careful with your maths here. You can use a calculator to help with your answers.

If you have time, use two different methods of calculation, in order to check your answer.

....
....
....
....
....
....
....
....
....
....
....
....
....
....
....
....
....
....
....
....
....
....
....
....

(b) State the error in the HTML code below and explain how it can be resolved.

3 marks

```
<td width="784" valign="top" class="Body4"><p><strong>Party</strong>)
    prices for catering
</td>
</p>
```

Remember that every HTML code tag needs to be paired.

....

....

....

....

....

....

....

The HTML code that Kerri wrote to show cake prices on her website can be seen in Section 3 of the information sheets on page 36.

(c) Explain how the **three** errors in this HTML script can be corrected.

6 marks

Errors in the HTML can be a result of inconsistent naming of objects and calculation methods.

1 ....

....

....

....

2 ....

....

....

....

3 ....

....

....

....

(d) Evaluate techniques which can be used to help maintain the code.

12 marks

Make sure you structure your work carefully and include as many relevant points as you can think of.

....

....

....

....

....

....

....

....

....

....

....

....

....

....

....

....

....

....

....

....

....

....

....

....

Total for Revision Question 4 = 27 marks

END OF REVISION TEST 2

TOTAL FOR REVISION TEST 2 = 90 MARKS

Information for Revision test 2

The information below should be used to answer some of the revision questions on pages 22–33. The information is divided into three sections, with each section relating to a specific revision question. The details of the actual exam may change, so always make sure you are up to date. Ask your tutor or check the Pearson website for the most up-to-date Sample Assessment Material to get an idea of the structure of your exam and what this requires of you.

SECTION 1

Links The information in this section should be used to answer Revision Question 1(a) on page 22.

Figure 1 shows a design for the Level 1 screen from the game.

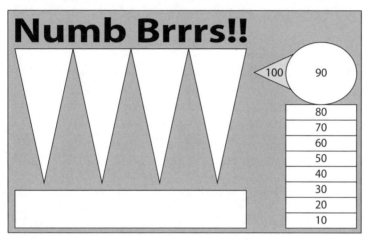

Figure 1

This game is designed to help the user practise their maths. The white box at the bottom of the screen will contain a mathematical calculation with four possible answers shown in the triangles, from which the user can choose the answer they think is correct.

The scoring boxes to the right of the screen are not visible at the start; they show with each correct answer. An incorrect answer removes the last score box from view, as in this example:

Answers	Score boxes showing
Correct	10
Correct	10/20
Incorrect	10
Correct	10/20
Correct	10/20/30
Correct	10/20/30/40

SECTION 2

 Links The information in this section should be used to answer Revision Questions 2(f) on page 27, and 2(g) on page 28.

Figure 2 shows the pseudocode for the bed and breakfast booking system. The pseudocode validates ranges of reference codes.

```
BEGIN
ValidEntry = False
IF left 3 characters of DataEntry = AAD
    IF right 3 characters of DataEntry >= 400
        ValidEntry = True
IF left 3 characters of DataEntry = CSD
    IF right 3 characters of DataEntry >= 200
        IF right 3 characters of DataEntry < 600
            ValidEntry = True
IF left 3 characters of DataEntry = GTH
    IF right 3 characters of DataEntry < 200
        ValidEntry = True
    IF right 3 characters of DataEntry >= 600
        IF right 3 characters of DataEntry < 800
            ValidEntry = True
IF left 3 characters of DataEntry = WWS
    IF right 3 characters of DataEntry > 399
        ValidEntry = True
END
```

Figure 2

SECTION 3

> **Links** The information in this section should be used to answer Revision Question 4(c) on page 32.

Figure 3 shows the HTML code that Kerri wrote to show cake prices on her website.

1	`<script>`
2	`  function calculate(form) {`
3	`    var price = 5;`
4	`    if (form.elements.icing.checked)`
5	`      price += 1;`
6	`    if (form.elements.cherrys.checked)`
7	`      price -= 2;`
8	`    if (form.elements.fruit.checked)`
9	`      price += 1;`
10	`    if (form.elements.writing.checked)`
11	`      price += 2.5;`
12	`    form.elements.result.value = price;`
13	`  }`
14	`</script>`
15	`<form name="pricecalc" onsubmit="return false" onchange="calculate(this)">`
16	`  <fieldset>`
17	`   <legend>Work out the price of each cake</legend>`
18	`   <p>Base cost: £5.</p>`
19	`   <p>Select additional options:</p>`
20	`   <ul>`
21	`    <li><label><input type=checkbox name=icing> Pink icing (£1)</label></li>`
22	`    <li><label><input type=checkbox name=cherries> Cherries (£2)</label></li>`
23	`    <li><label><input type=checkbox name=fruit> Fruit (£1.50)</label></li>`
24	`    <li><label><input type=checkbox name=writing> Individualised writing (£2.50)</label></li>`
25	`   </ul>`
26	`   <p>Total: £<output name=result></output></p>`
27	`  </fieldset>`
28	`  <script>`
29	`   calculate(document.forms.pricecalc);`
30	`  </script>`
31	`</form>`

Figure 3

Unit 2:
Fundamentals of Computer Systems

Your exam

Unit 2 will be assessed through an exam, which will be set by Pearson. You will need to use your knowledge and understanding of how computer systems work, including the role of hardware and software, the way components of a system work together and how data in a system is used. You then respond to questions that require short and long answers.

Your Revision Workbook

This workbook is designed to **revise skills** that might be needed in your exam. The selected content, outcomes, questions and answers are provided to help you to revise content and ways of applying your skills. Ask your tutor or check the **Pearson website** for the most up-to-date **Sample Assessment Material** and **Mark Scheme** to get an indication of the structure of your actual exam and what this requires of you, and whether you can use a calculator in the exam. The details of the actual exam may change so always make sure you are up to date.

To support your revision, this workbook contains revision questions to help you revise the skills that might be needed in your exam.

Your response to the questions will help you to revise:
- hardware and software
- computer architecture
- how data is represented by computer systems
- how data is organised on computer systems
- how data is transmitted by computer systems
- the use of logic and data flow in computer systems.

> **Links** To help you revise skills that might be needed in your Unit 2 exam, this workbook contains two sets of revision questions starting on pages 38 and 51. The first is guided and models good techniques, to help you develop your skills. The second gives you the opportunity to apply the skills you have developed. See the introduction on page iii for more information on features included to help you revise.

Revision test 1

To support your revision, the questions below help you to revise the skills that you might need in your exam. The revision test is divided into four questions, each based on a different scenario. The details of the actual exam may change, so always make sure you are up to date. Ask your tutor or check the Pearson website for the most up-to-date Sample Assessment Material to get an idea of the structure of your exam and what this requires of you.

1 A major amplifier manufacturer has decided to create a wi-fi hi-fi system. This will allow users to search music streaming services they are subscribed to and play selected tracks wirelessly on the company's system.

(a) Draw a diagram of the data structure the system will use for streaming the data from the music services.

2 marks

> Your sketch should include both how data is stored and also how it is accessed.

Each track found can be added straight away to the system and all tracks played in the order they have been added.

(b) Explain which data structure will be used by the programmers to implement this.   **2 marks**

A queue is the most suitable data structure because ....

....

....

....

When tracks have been selected they are displayed in the order they are to be played. The whole collection of tracks can be named and saved to be accessed later. This collection can be added to, deleted from, and sorted by artist, album, track or date added.

(c) State which data structure will be used by the programmers to implement this.   **1 mark**

....

> 🔗 **Links** If you are not sure of the answer, revise Data structures (1) in the Revision Guide, page 76.

Remember to read all parts of a question before answering each part. The answer to 1(d), for example, may give you a clue to the answer to 1(c).

(d) Give the name that music services usually give to this collection of tracks. `1 mark`

> Think of iTunes, Spotify, Deezer, Sonos, etc.

....

A specialised Harvard processor is to be used for the CPU for the main streaming device.

(e) Complete the diagram below which shows the way the Harvard architecture deals
with memory. `2 marks`

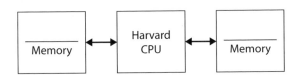

Memory ⟷ Harvard CPU ⟷ Memory

> **Links** Revise Alternative architectures in the Revision Guide, page 68.

(f) Describe the type of operating system that would be appropriate for this device. `2 marks`

....

....

....

....

> **Links** Revise Operating systems in the Revision Guide, pages 56, 57 and 59.

Part of the electronics for the system box requires that a circuit be implemented for the Boolean
expression A.B + B.C

Guided

(g) Complete the truth table below for this expression. `4 marks`

A	B	C	A.B	B.C	A.B + B.C
0	0	0			

A, B, C should be filled in as binary numbers between 0 and 7, with A as the MSB and C as the LSB, i.e. row 1 is 000 (0), row 2 is 001 (1), … row 8 is 111 (7).

A.B should be a 1 if A and B both have 1s, otherwise it is 0.

A.B+B.C: Remember the AND (e.g. A.B) must be performed before the OR(+) so, in this case, simply OR together the previous two columns. If there is a 1 in either column then the result is a 1.

> Guided

(h) Complete the circuit diagram below.

4 marks

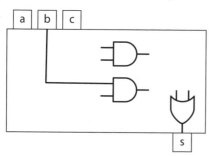

Use a ruler and a pencil. Draw straight lines for the connections.

The b input is going to both AND gates, so draw a vertical line from b down to level with the top input of the bottom AND gate and draw a horizontal line across to this input. Then draw another line from b to the bottom input of the top AND gate. Then complete a similar task for the a and c inputs.

🔗 **Links** Revise Boolean logic in the Revision Guide, page 88.

Total for Revision Question 1 = 18 marks

2 | Cookie & Co. manufactures cookies and cakes. The factory is a secure building to ensure the best hygiene and security practices. Entry to all factory areas requires an authorisation card with a magnetic stripe which identifies the user and must be used at each entry point. The card system maintains records of who is in the factory at a given time and for how long. This data is kept available for internal factory inspectors as part of their audit of security.

Guided

(a) Explain how this card system ensures that only staff or authorised visitors enter the factory.

2 marks

The magnetic stripe on the card contains identification data. ....

....

....

....

(b) State **one** weakness in this system.

1 mark

Any non-biometric ID measure will share this weakness to some extent.

....

....

....

Guided

(c) Describe a different scheme that Cookie & Co. could use to authorise entry, with separate access methods for staff and for visitors.

4 marks

State a method and describe how it would work both for staff (for whom biometrics are viable) and visitors (where they are not).

Biometric fingerprint scan for .... This would mean ....

....

....

This involves using a camera to ....

....

....

Visitors would ....

....

Guided

(d) Discuss the procedures Cookie & Co. should use to backup and archive this data and the requirements for this.

8 marks

Start by defining backup and archiving. Make it clear what the differences are between them and then list a set of procedures that may be undertaken.

Backing up involves making a copy of ....

....

....

....

....

....

Archiving is a different process. It is not concerned with live data but ....

....

....

....

....

....

It is important to have a standard set of procedures that is documented and followed without fail.

A possible set of procedures would be:

....

....

....

....

....

....

....

....

....

....

....

....

Cookie & Co. has a factory shop where they sell baked products directly to the public. Figure 1 is an extract from a spreadsheet showing the number of cookies and cakes sold by each worker in the 3 months between January and March. The cost of a cookie is £2 and a cake is £3.

	Worker 1				Worker 2				Price in £	
	Number sold									
	Jan	Feb	Mar		Jan	Feb	Mar			
Cookies	10	20	10		4	3	4		cookies	2
Cakes	5	6	5		3	4	4		cake	3

Figure 1

Guided

(e) Using matrix addition, calculate the totals each worker has sold.

2 marks

$$\begin{bmatrix} 10 & 20 & 10 \\ 5 & 6 & 5 \end{bmatrix} + \begin{bmatrix} 4 & 3 & 4 \\ 3 & 4 & 4 \end{bmatrix} = \begin{bmatrix} 10+4 & 20+3 & 10+4 \\ \dots & \dots & \dots \end{bmatrix}$$

$$= \begin{bmatrix} 14 & \dots & \dots \\ \dots & 10 & \dots \end{bmatrix}$$

Complete the answer above. When asked to make calculations, remember to show your working.

Guided

(f) Transpose the matrix of prices.

1 mark

$$\begin{bmatrix} 2 \\ 3 \end{bmatrix}^T = \begin{bmatrix} \dots & \dots \end{bmatrix}$$

Transposing is changing vertical to horizontal (or horizontal to vertical). Complete the second set of brackets above.

Guided

(g) Using matrix multiplication, calculate the total revenues for each of January, February and March.

4 marks

$$\begin{bmatrix} \dots & \dots \end{bmatrix}\begin{bmatrix} 14 & \dots & \dots \\ \dots & 10 & \dots \end{bmatrix} = \begin{bmatrix} 14\times\dots & \dots\times\dots & \dots\times\dots \\ + & + & + \\ \dots\times\dots & 10\times\dots & \dots\times\dots \end{bmatrix}$$

$$= \begin{bmatrix} \dots & \dots & \dots \end{bmatrix}$$

The revenue would be £.................. for January, £.................. for February and £..................
for March.

Complete the answer above. You can use the answers from 2(e) and 2(f) to calculate this quickly.

If you have time, double check the answer by multiplying the figures. Use a calculator.

Links Revise Indices and matrices in the Revision Guide, page 78.

Total for Revision Question 2 = 22 marks

3 Reskey is building his own computer system to act as a media and games centre in his home. He has bought a tower case and a motherboard with six expansion slots, a compatible dual core CPU, a power supply and a fan. As he wants it to function as a media centre and do fast graphics for games, he has also bought a separate graphics adapter. He also has a 1 TB hard disc to store his videos and games on. For input/output (I/O) he has bought a touch screen display and a mouse.

> Guided

(a) State the other main internal hardware component that he needs to acquire to make it a functioning computer and explain why it is needed.

2 marks

> Always take note of every element of the question. This revision question asks about internal components of the computer system.

RAM because ....

....

....

> 🔗 **Links** For information on Internal components, see the Revision Guide, page 51.

The motherboard manual mentions the system bus.

> Guided

(b) Describe what the system bus does.

3 marks

> The system bus is a shorthand notation for three separate buses. State what they are.

The system bus is a combination of ....

....

....

....

....

Reskey's friends have told him he can speed up the clock to achieve a faster processor.

(c) State whether this is a viable option.

2 marks

> State the positive effect that speeding up the clock will have on the speed of operations. Then state the potential problem. Whenever possible, a balanced answer will always be best. The revision question is worth 2 marks so therefore give 2 factors.

....

....

....

....

....

The CPU has a number of special registers – accumulator, CIR (Current Instruction Register), MAR (Memory Address Register), MDR (Memory Data Register) and PC program counter.

> Guided

(d) Describe the role of each register in the fetch execute cycle.

8 marks

FETCH:

Contents of PC copied to MAR

....

....

....

....

DECODE:

Decode instruction held by the CIR.

....

EXECUTE:

The opcode identifies the type of instruction it is and control unit controls execution

....

....

....

stored in ....

If instruction is a jump then .... is updated with the jump address.

Links To complete this answer, revise The fetch decode execute cycle in the Revision Guide, page 67.

Reskey has decided to buy an open source operating system based on a free distribution of Unix. This is because he can buy software that can emulate two of the major proprietary operating systems and he hopes that this will allow him to play the latest games designed for both of these systems.

> **Guided** >

(e) Evaluate Reskey's decision.

10 marks

> The introduction should set up the rest of the answer. In this case, a possible approach is to state the circumstances in which an emulator may work. This can be used to contrast with situations where it is less successful.

It is possible to emulate other systems using an emulator. Software is available on Unix systems that can emulate other proprietary systems, such as Windows systems or Apple Macintosh systems, whose kernel is itself based on a distribution of Unix.

If the CPU that is used for the proprietary system is the same or slower and less complex than the system running the software, the emulation can potentially be quite successful.

> Now relate the answer to the technical details of the case. These include the basic computer system and CPU used, and also the operating systems used for the source and target systems. How effective could this be? What would be the constraints?

Next, deal with the major issue that Reskey wants to emulate games. What special requirements do games make of the CPU, of graphics processors, and so on? What special problems will arise as a result of this?

....

....

....

....

....

....

....

....

....

....

....

....

....

....

....

....

....

....

....

....

What are the implications of the input/output hardware used in games?

....

....

....

....

....

....

....

....

....

....

....

....

....

....

....

....

....

....

....

....

> Conclude with a summary of the main points made. As it is an evaluation question, include a final recommendation.

In summary, the idea of using this system under Unix to emulate other advanced proprietary systems, particularly those running CPU and GPU intensive software which requires specialist I/O hardware, is not really a viable option. At best, it would allow a flavour of the games and, at worst, they would not play.

Total for Revision Question 3 = 25 marks

4 VeloWhere is planning to introduce to the market a GPS system for cyclists called Velo2Go. It will be a portable device that can be attached to the handlebars and allow route planning and location finding on the move. It can be removed from the handlebars for updating and communicating with other devices. The device will receive a GPS signal to update its current position.

(a) Identify what type of channel GPS is.

`1 mark`

> The answer is either Simplex, Duplex or Half-duplex. To decide which one it is, consider whether the data travels in more than one direction and if so, can it be passed both ways at once?

....

VeloWhere is intending to license maps data from a major supplier to be displayed in full colour on the touch screen display. The user will log on from their computer system and the maps data will be downloaded over the internet from the main maps server in the USA using standard TCP/IP protocols. The Velo2Go has a serial adapter that allows fast serial communication via a standard USB port. This is plugged into the computer, completes a handshake procedure, sends its registered code which comprises 2 extended ASCII alphabetical characters and 4 BCD digits to the PC, and the data is downloaded to the device automatically using serial communications.

(b) Describe the purpose of a handshake.

`2 marks`

....

....

....

....

> 🔗 **Links** Revise Data communications channels in the Revision Guide, page 80.

Guided

(c) Assuming the registration code a device sends is 0101 0110 0110 0101 0110 1001 1001 0001 identify the code as written in English on the box.

`4 marks`

0101 0110 ....

0110 0101 ....

0110 ....

1001 ....

1001 ....

0001 ....

> First split the data into the appropriate lengths for decoding (i.e. two ASCII characters) (8 bits each) and 4 BCD digits (4 bits each):
>
> The first two are ASCII so the first digits define the type of data; 010 is upper case and 011 is lower case:
> **010**10110 is the _nd letter of the alphabet in **upper case**
> **011**00101 is the _th letter of the alphabet in **lower case**
>
> 0110 in BCD is a 4-digit binary conversion, so it is 0+4+2+0=6
> 1001
> 0001

The code transmitted is ....

Guided

(d) Explain what each of the following elements of a packet refer to and how they are used in this case: source address, destination address, payload, sequence number and a checksum.

8 marks

> Try to use details from the scenario, such as the server in California, the user's PC, and the maps data to relate your answer, as well as possible, to the case.

Source address

The address (IP address) of the server in California from which the maps data is sent.

Destination address

....

....

....

Payload

....

....

....

Sequence number

....

....

....

Checksum

....

....

....

> **Links** Revise Data transmission protocols in the Revision Guide, page 82.

Total for Revision Question 4 = 15 marks

END OF REVISION TEST 1

TOTAL FOR REVISION TEST = 80 MARKS

Revision test 2

To support your revision, the questions below help you to revise the skills that you might need in your exam. The revision test is divided into four questions, each based on a different scenario. The details of the actual exam may change, so always make sure you are up to date. Ask your tutor or check the Pearson website for the most up-to-date Sample Assessment Material to get an idea of the structure of your exam and what this requires of you.

1 | PAT Ltd runs a grocery and news cornershop chain across a busy suburban area. It is looking to upgrade its computer systems across the whole chain to deal with the till system and also the accounting, marketing and CCTV security.

(a) State **two** reasons why a 'menu-based' interface could be chosen over a full GUI for the till system.

2 marks

Reason 1.

....

....

....

Reason 2.

....

....

....

Links Revise Operating systems (3) in the Revision Guide, page 59.

PAT Ltd wants to use a flatbed barcode scanner to scan the EAN codes on the groceries, newspapers, books and magazines, as in large supermarkets.

(b) Describe the principles of how the scanner reads the bar code.

4 marks

....

....

....

....

....

....

....

....

....

....

The rightmost digit of the bar code is a check digit.

(c) Describe a check digit and how is it used to perform error checking.

2 marks

....

....

....

....

Links Find out more about Input and output devices and Error detection in the Revision Guide, pages 52, 53 and 86.

(d) State another input device which could be used to enter product data at the point of sale.

1 mark

....

Links Revise Data processing in the Revision Guide, page 64.

The company wants a full HD colour CCTV system for each of the stores. The CCTV will be streamed to the local system and backed up daily to a NAS device configured with dual disc RAID 1 storage. This will be held in the main store and be accessible to the other stores securely over the internet.

(e) Describe **two** advantages of a NAS for this purpose.

4 marks

1 ....

....

....

....

2 ....

....

....

....

Links Revise Data storage and recovery in the Revision Guide, page 55.

(f) Describe **one** major advantage and **one** disadvantage of using RAID 1 configuration for this purpose.

4 marks

> Consider what RAID 1 does, such as having an immediate advantage in case of failure but with the disadvantage of a large expense. Explain each advantage and disadvantage in more detail.

Advantage:

....

....

....

....

Disadvantage:

....

....

....

....

(g) Evaluate the alternative of running a five-disc RAID 5 configuration to store the CCTV data and other important shared media.

8 marks

....

....

....

....

....

....

....

....

....

....

....

....

....

....

....

....

....

Total for Revision Question 1 = 25 marks

2 Petunia Garden Palace is an e-commerce store selling plants and garden supplies. When an e-commerce retailer takes credit card details from a customer it usually stores and transmits the credit card data itself using symmetric key encryption technology. The customer's browser will negotiate with the store's server the exact standard that will be used (usually using the most secure that both are capable of, such as DES 56 bit, CAST 128 bit, AES 256 bit).

(a) Give **two** reasons why symmetric key encryption is used rather than any other form of encryption to store the confidential data.

2 marks

Reason 1.

....

....

Reason 2.

....

....

Links Find out about Encryption in modern computer systems in the Revision Guide, page 84.

A digital certificate shows that an encrypted web connection identity is from who it says it is, that is, it is valid. Figure 1 shows the certificate authority.

Certificate

General

Certificate information

This certificate is intended for the following purpose(s):
- Ensures the identity of a remote computer
- Proves your identity to a remote computer
- 1.11.753.1.2456689.2.1
- 1.74.246.2.1.1

Issued to: designco.com

Issued by: Digiserver CA

Valid from: 14/06/2017 to 24/10/2020

OK

Figure 1

(b) Explain why the same technology will not work for establishing a secure connection between the client and the store's server.

2 marks

Consider how the key would be passed between the two parties.

....

....

....

....

....

....

The digital certificate behind the padlock on encrypted connections from the web store provides proof that the user can trust the domain name and the public key for the site that the user is connected to.

(c) Explain how the customer's browser will use this public key to establish a secure connection with the server that is hosting the secure page.

6 marks

....

....

....

....

....

....

....

....

....

....

....

....

....

....

....

Petunia Garden Palace (PGP) uses two main sources of images.

They hire a professional photographer to take very high quality photographs of their plants and supplies using a DSLR camera capable of taking photographs of up to 8688 x 5792 pixels. The full resolution images are stored on the server as RAW images for use on display boards, print and poster advertising etc. as these images are suitable for printing as an A0 image at a resolution of 200 dpi. Selected photos are copied and converted and then stored in two different sizes for display as thumbnails and also as full screen images on the e-commerce website.

They also hire the services of an illustrator who draws beautiful sketches of plants and plant settings to add variety to the website, and also draws 3D sketches and plans of the garden buildings and hard landscaping they supply to be used in instruction manuals and online help. These are stored as vector drawings on the server and then converted to the appropriate format when they are used on the website.

(d) Name the format that is most appropriate for storing the converted photographs for the web.

1 mark

....

Links Revise Image representation and Compression in the Revision Guide, pages 75 and 85.

(e) Name the format which is most appropriate for storing the converted illustrations for the web.

[1 mark]

....

(f) Discuss why PGP should retain the original photograph files as well as storing two new versions of them, rather than just keep one file.

[6 marks]

> Consider why the original file format is useful and under what circumstances it would not be useful or usable. Then consider the advantages and disadvantages of the two web-format files.

....

....

....

....

....

....

....

....

....

....

....

....

....

(g) Explain why it makes sense to retain the illustration files separately rather than photograph them at a high resolution and then store them with the other photographs.

[2 marks]

> Consider the advantages and disadvantages of the type of format of an illustration and apply them to this case.

....

....

....

....

....

....

Total for Revision Question 2 = 20 marks

3 Figure 2 shows a diagram of a computer system architecture.

(a) Complete the diagram in Figure 2 to show clearly each component (I/O controller, CPU), each connection between them and the direction of connection.

4 marks

What is the clock part of? Consider which buses are bidirectional and which unidirectional.

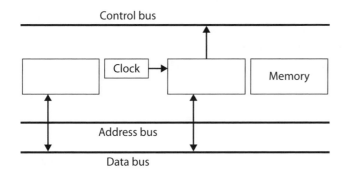

Control bus

Clock

Memory

Address bus

Data bus

Figure 2

Links To help you answer this revision question, revise Approaches to computer architecture and The fetch decode execute cycle in the Revision Guide, pages 66 and 67.

(b) Describe the role of the clock in a typical Von Neumann stored program architecture.

2 marks

....

....

....

....

Links Revise The fetch decode execute cycle, Alternative architectures and Parallel computing for the following questions. See the Revision Guide, pages 66, 67 and 69.

(c) Explain the implications on performance of speeding up the clock.

2 marks

....

....

....

....

(d) Discuss the use of cluster computing and multi-core processing as strategies for overcoming the Von Neumann bottleneck.

12 marks

> There are 12 marks available to you in this revision question. A full discussion is required. Make at least 6 major expanded points with an argument running through the answer, always remembering to relate it to the question.
> - Start with a definition of the bottleneck.
> - Define cluster computing and multi-core processing and state that they are both potential strategies.
> - Give a detailed explanation of how cluster computing gives parallel distributed computing.
> - Give the advantages and disadvantages and relate them to the bottleneck.
> - Give a detailed explanation of how multi-core processing enables parallel computing.
> - Give the advantages and disadvantages and relate them to the bottleneck.
> - Summarise your argument in a conclusion.

....
....
....
....
....
....
....
....
....
....
....
....
....
....
....
....
....
....
....
....
....
(d) ....
....
....

....

....

....

....

....

....

....

....

....

....

....

....

....

....

....

....

....

....

Links Revise Parallel computing in particular in the Revision Guide, page 69.

Total for Revision Question 3 = 20 marks

4 | Longway Airport has an information system which displays the textual information of the gates and times of arrival and departures of all aeroplanes. Figure 3 shows the departures board.

Flight No.	Destination	Gate	Departure
EZ123	LGW	2	12:20
NG222	PMI	1	12:50
KA22	JFK	3	13:05
VIR101	LHW	4	13:15

Figure 3

(a) Identify the data processing function that has been completed on the information in Figure 3 prior to sending.

1 mark

Make sure your answer is detailed enough to make it obvious what you mean.

....

....

 Links Revise Data processing functions in the Revision Guide, page 65.

Textual data is transmitted between simpler systems at the airport using 7-bit ASCII code with a parity bit. Upper case 'A' is represented as 100 0001 in 7-bit binary ASCII code.

(b) Assuming that even parity has been set, calculate what the following message would say.

1100 1100
0100 0111
1101 0111

6 marks

Show your workings.

Even parity means there should be an even number of 1s, which there is in each of these cases, so only the last seven digits need to be considered. The first two digits define the type of character; 10 is an upper case letter. The last five digits give, in binary, the position of the letter in the alphabet.

....

....

....

....

 Links Revise Binary and number systems and Error detection in the Revision Guide, pages 70 and 86.

(c)   Explain what would happen if the next character received was 1100 0111.

1 mark

In this case, there is an odd number of 1s in the byte, so which error correction mechanism would be most appropriate here?

....

....

Links   Revise Error correction in the Revision Guide, page 87.

The details of arriving aircraft are entered into the Longway Runway Management System (LRMS) in the order they will be allowed to land by the airport controller. Resources for landing (landing bay, tow-truck, luggage handlers etc) are scheduled as they come to the front of the system and when they have safely landed and been dealt with, the aircraft are removed from the LRMS.

(d)   State what type of data structure would be most appropriate for the LRMS.

1 mark

....

Links   Revise Data structures in the Revision Guide, pages 76 and 77.

(e)   Describe the implications of this type of data structure for managing resources.

2 marks

....

....

....

....

(f) Describe what type of operating system (OS) would be most appropriate for aircraft and why.

`4 marks`

....

....

....

....

....

....

....

....

....

State which type of OS would be most suitable and give reasons why.

Consider:
- what the overriding concerns for operating a plane are.
- how the hardware in the plane is connected and controlled.
- what type of input hardware is most relevant.
- what type of OS meets these needs.

Links Revise Operating systems in the Revision Guide, pages 56, 57 and 59.

Total for Revision Question 4 = 15 marks

END OF REVISION TEST 2

TOTAL FOR REVISION TEST 2 = 80 MARKS

Unit 3: Planning and Management of Computing Projects

Your set task

Unit 3 will be assessed through a task, which will be set by Pearson. You will need to use your understanding of project planning and management concepts, applied to a computing project.

Your Revision Workbook

This workbook is designed to **revise skills** that might be needed in your assessed task. The selected content, outcomes, questions and answers are provided to help you revise content and ways of applying your skills. Ask your tutor or check the **Pearson website** for the most up-to-date **Sample Assessment Material** and **Mark Scheme** to get an idea of the structure of your assessed task and what this requires of you. Make sure you check the details in relation to completing work on a computer, any templates that may be provided, and use of a calculator. The details of the actual assessed task may change so always make sure you are up to date.

To support your revision, this workbook contains revision tasks to help you revise the skills that might be needed in your set task.

Your response to the tasks will help you to revise the production of:

- a Project Initiation Document using a given document
- the following project planning documentation based on the information provided in the computing project scenario:
  - a Gantt chart
  - a resource list
  - a cost plan
- a Project Checkpoint Report for your project, using a given document
- an email to send to the project sponsor using your company's email document.

Links To help you revise skills that might be needed in your Unit 3 set task, this workbook contains two revision tasks starting on pages 65 and 88. The first is guided and models good techniques, to help you develop your skills. The second gives you the opportunity to apply the skills you have developed. See the introduction on page iii for more information on features included to help you revise.

Revision task 1

To support your revision, the task below helps you to revise the skills that you might need in your assessed task. The revision task consists of four activities based on a task brief. Electronic templates of a **Project Initiation Document**, **Project Checkpoint Report** and **Project Email** for use with the revision task (activities 1, 3 and 4) are available to download (see pages 68, 81 and 105 for information on how to access each of these).

The details of the actual assessed task may change, so always make sure you are up to date. Ask your tutor or check the Pearson website for the most up-to-date Sample Assessment Material to get an idea of the structure of your assessed task and what this requires of you.

Revision task brief – part 1

You are asked to use your project planning and management understanding and skills within a given computing project scenario.

You are the Project Manager at a major training provider that offers a range of courses in first aid, fire safety training, health and safety, and food hygiene, to businesses, organisations and individuals. Your Managing Director has allocated you to an in-house project to design and implement a new training recording system.

In the first part of the revision task, you will need to complete project documentation to initiate and launch a project to design and implement a new training recording system. In the second part of the task, you will monitor and control the project's progress to its completion and closure.

Read the information that follows. You will then use page 68 forward to make notes and complete Revision activity 1, and page 77 forward to make notes and complete Revision activity 2.

Information

The business case has been prepared, and a budget of £80 000 has been set aside for the project.

It has been decided to implement the system using direct changeover.

The company is closed for annual holidays on 1–31 August, and the system must be up and running ready for the training team's return to work on 1 September.

The new online system will consist of the following six modules:

- Course schedule module interface with business logic (five functional points)
- Payment module (two functional points)
- Trainer/Assessor module (three functional points)
- Venue module (three functional points)
- Client services (three functional points)
- Reporting module (three complex functional points).

A Business Analyst has been allocated to the project and will work with the Training Manager to carry out an analysis of the current paper-based and electronic systems and create the requirements specifications. This is estimated to take three days.

The company uses a paper diary to record dates of training courses, a database to record the Trainer/Assessors' details, another database to record the clients' details and a manual accounts system. The Managing Director wants to integrate and automate all of the systems. In the second stage of the project, the company is planning to offer online courses, where organisations and individuals will be able to book and pay for courses online.

The Business Analyst and Software Team Manager will work together to design the new system. Three days have been allocated to the project design stage.

A Webpage Developer, a Software Developer and a Software Tester have also been allocated to your team.

The Software Team Manager will monitor the Software Developer's and the Webpage Developer's development of the new system. A Software Tester will also be involved in the development stage, which has been allocated 16 days.

The Training Manager will update the Course Schedule database in preparation for the new training recording system and will work closely with the Webpage Developer, who is currently completing a website development course.

The Software Team Manager has asked the Software Tester to use ISO/IEC 25010:2011 standard to test the new system, a methodology that the tester has not used before.

As the training provider does not have the skilled staff to manage the project or design and develop the system, it has been decided to hire a local server contractor, who will design and build the server and computers, install the system and software and maintain it.

The Finance Director, who will act as the client for this project, has received a quotation and agreed costs with a local server contractor.

Quotation from server contractor:
- Server hardware £2300
- Microsoft Windows server £2750
- Microsoft SQL server £2356
- Web development software £510
- Microsoft Office £167

All work is fully guaranteed for 12 months.

In addition, as the training company's IT team is understaffed, the server contractor is to supply a Software Developer to support the design stage of the project. The Finance Director agreed the additional cost of £600 on 12 July.

The system will be installed on 29 August.

System installations costs have been agreed at £850. The installation will take three days.

The Training Manager and Software Team Manager will support system installations in the quality checking process to ensure that the new system works as expected.

The Finance Director has asked for weekly email reports on risk assessments, Project Checkpoint and work package tolerance status and a weekly email to all company managers informing them of the project status.

The new online training system should:
- allow a client to book a course online
- send an invoice to the client's email address for payment for the course
- link to the course database
- link the client database and trainer database to the company accounts system.

The training provider receives many phone calls from clients either requesting training or providing updated information, such as a new address or change of name, and it would like clients to be able to update their own details online.

The Training Manager has asked one of the Trainer/Assessors to help with the project analysis, design and testing stage. The Trainer/Assessor will arrange some meetings with clients to ask them what they would like the system to do, and to send questionnaires to the larger companies who book courses.

The Software Team Manager has also asked the Trainer/Assessor to use user acceptance testing as part of the quality and review process.

The acceptance testing has been estimated to take five days in total prior to the implementation stage of the project.

The Finance Director has calculated staff costs information, per person, to help with the project's budget planning:
- Project Manager £50 per hour
- Business Analyst £48 per hour
- Software Team Manager £42 per hour
- Software Developer £32 per hour
- Webpage Developer £32 per hour
- Software Tester £25 per hour
- Training Manager £39 per hour
- Trainer/Assessor £24 per hour

During the duration of the project all staff work a 5-day week, 6.5 hours per day, for 31 days.

The Finance Director has provided additional responsibility costs per function point to help you plan the project.

Role	Hours per function point	Notes
Software Team Manager	2	Responsible for software and webpage development; additional cost for helping with the testing stage
Software Developer	1	Responsible for software development; additional cost for helping with the testing stage
Webpage Developer	0.5	Responsible for webpage development; additional cost for helping with the testing stage
Software Tester	0.5	Responsible for testing the functionality of the programme

Equipment rental	Pro-rata cost per 6.5-hour day	Notes
Software Team Manager	£24	27" LED screen for 31 days
Software Developer	£19	24" LED screen for 31 days
Webpage Developer	£24	27" LED screen for 31 days
Software Tester	£19	24" LED screen for 31 days

Four laptop computers, each costing £699, will be purchased for the Project Manager, Business Analyst, Software Tester and Trainer/Assessor to use on the project.

Company structure:

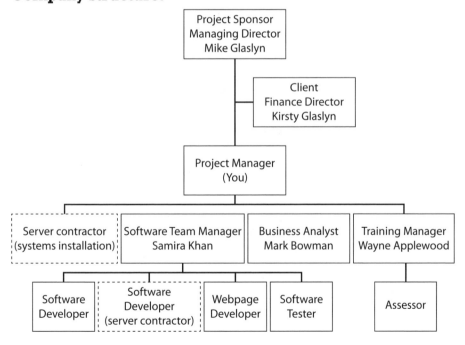

Revision task

The details of the actual set task may change, so always make sure you are up to date. Ask your tutor or check the Pearson website for the most up-to-date Sample Assessment Material to get an idea of the structure of your set task and what this requires of you.

All the documents in this revision task should be produced using a computer. You will need to save your documents using the formats and naming conventions indicated.

> **Guided**

Revision activity 1

Produce a Project Initiation Document (PID) for your project using the document provided.

You can access a template of a Project Initiation Document (PID) for use in Revision task 1, Revision activity 1 by scanning this link with your smartphone or tablet and downloading the file called revisiontaskPID1.docx. Alternatively, go to the following link: http://activetea.ch/2wN3dui and save the file on your laptop or computer ready for you to input information as you complete the revision activity.

Add further lines to the Project Initiation Document sections if required.

The business case has already been populated. Option 2 (design and build a system using external skilled staff and subcontract support to an external computer system support company) has been chosen for this project.

You should take some time to read and understand the revision task brief, information and the tasks you are to complete. You may find it helpful to make notes to use as you complete the project documentation.

Read the revision task brief. Jot down relevant information:

Project title

Project sponsor

Client name

Key dates

Stakeholders (internal and external)

Project aims and SMART objectives

Budget and costs

Project Initiation Document

Project details

Project title	Training Recording System
Project Sponsor name	
Client name	
Project Manager name	Your name
Start date	1 August 2017
Completion date	
Estimated cost	

Complete the project details. Make sure that the information from the scenario is entered accurately, with all sections fully completed.

You can find all of the information in the scenario. Use the notes that you made in the revision activity to help you.

 Links The Project Initiation Document (PID) identifies for stakeholders all the key management information required to get the project started. To find out more about the PID, see the Revision Guide, pages 129–132.

Document details

Version	Modifications	Author	Date
2	Project budget update: Software Developer additional cost		

The modifications carried out in the PID are recorded in the document details section. The first approved version of a document is version 1.

The 'Modifications' are a brief summary of any changes made to the document.

The 'Author' of the document updated the document details.

You should consider all of the project management documents and read the scenario carefully to see if they have been updated.

Document approvals

This document requires the following approvals:

Name	Role	Signature	Date	Version
Kirsty Glaslyn	Finance Director	Kirsty Glaslyn	July	2

Who are the key stakeholders who approve the project?

Read the scenario carefully and record their names and roles. You may have various versions of the PID that require approval.

All sections should be fully completed.

The information entered should be relevant and accurate.

 Links For a reminder about who stakeholders are see the Revision Guide, page 110.

> **Guided**

Document distribution

This document has been distributed to:

Name	Role	Date of Issue	Version
Mike Glaslyn	Managing Director	July	2

In the document distribution section, list the names and roles of the people who have been sent the document. Consider both internal and external stakeholders.

> **Guided**

Purpose of the Project Initiation Document

Project aims:

To provide an integrated system that will allow the training provider to record details of course, Trainer/Assessor and client.

To enable customers to search, book and pay for courses online.

....

....

....

Detailed project aims should be taken directly from the scenario; think about what the project is intended to do.

....

....

....

....

....

....

Guided

Project management and control:

Acceptance testing as part of the quality and review process. Tester/Assessor to use user acceptance testing as part of the quality and review process

Software Tester to use .... to test the new system

....

....

....

....

> Think about the project management controls relating to resources and finance that are available to the Project Manager. Also consider the quality assurance process.

Links For a reminder about Quality assurance process, see Revision Guide, page 102.

Guided

Background to the proposed work

The company does not have the facility for organisations and individuals to search for courses, book and pay for courses online.

Manual system is ....

....

....

> The scenario will identify the reason for the project. Make sure you provide as much detailed and relevant information as possible.

The modifications carried out in the PID are recorded in the document details section. The first approved version of a document is version 1.

The 'Modifications' are a brief summary of any changes made to the document.

The 'Author' of the document updated the document details.

You should consider all of the project management documents and read the scenario carefully to see if they have been updated.

Guided

Objectives

SMART Objective	Achieved?	Date and comments
Project start date 1 August	Yes	Project started successfully on 1 August
Project launch 1 September	Yes	
System installed 29 August		

Complete the SMART objectives for the project, whether they have been achieved and when. Provide as much detail as you can when listing each specific objective.

Links SMART objectives should be specific, measurable, achievable, realistic and time bound and must be relevant to the given scenario. For information on SMART objectives, see the Revision Guide, page 103.

> **Guided**

Scope

Organisations and individuals to book and pay for courses online

Integrate and automate all of the systems

....

....

....

....

....

....

The scope must clearly define what the project will and will not cover and its limitations.

Consider any internal and external influences, and resource- and staff-related issues.

Business case

The business case was prepared by the Finance Director.

The current system will not support the training resource system requirements.

There are two options:

1. buy a ready-made product and install and maintain it using existing internal staff

2. design and build a system using external skilled staff and subcontract support to an external computer system support company.

It has been agreed that option 2 is the preferred method.

The expected business benefit of the project is a measurable improvement in course sales, customer satisfaction and an integrated system that will reduce errors.

The new system is expected to:

- increase course occupancy to at least 95 per cent within the first six months
- improve client satisfaction to 90 per cent
- reduce administrative costs by 10 per cent within the next three months
- improve accuracy as a result of automated processes
- improve the Training Manager's reporting on course occupancy
- show Trainer/Assessors' availability in the electronic diary.

Timescale: The project should begin on 1 August and launch on 1 September when the training company reopens for business.

On 29 August the direct system implementation will begin for the Training Recording System.

The allocated budget for this project is £80 000 and the Finance Director expects a return of at least £1500 at the end of one year and an increase in course sales revenue of at least 20 per cent.

The Finance Director has identified the following major risks:

- retraining of staff to enable them to use the new integrated system efficiently
- lack of in-house technical expertise to maintain the system
- legal issues relating to security of Trainer/Assessor and client data
- budget constraints
- current hardware not capable of processing all of the data
- the lack of a contingency plan
- ongoing support costs.

Assumptions

Assumption	Validated by	Status	Comments
The staff will be able to use the new system	Training manager	Marginal	Additional training will be given

Complete the assumptions for the project by listing each one and who validated it. Comment on the status of the assumption.

Consider internal and external influences, resources, staff and quality standards.

Status may be marginal.

Links Early in the project, the Project Manager will have to make assumptions about possible risks and constraints that might affect its successful outcome. To find out more about the types of constraints that could affect a project, see the Revision Guide, page 111.

Constraints

Constraint	Validated by	Status	Comments
The service contractor will be able to supply the hardware and software within budget and quality	Software Team Manager	Critical	Alternative suppliers sourced to ensure that alternative hardware and software can be purchased within budget and of the required quality

Complete the constraint for the project by listing each one, who validated it and its status. Provide detailed comments on the status of the constraint.

Consider internal and external influences, resources, staff and quality standards.

Links A constraint is a limiting factor that may impact on the success of the project. See the Revision Guide, page 111, for more information on constraints.

Risk management strategy

Risk	Probability	Impact	Severity	Contingency Plan
The server contractor goes bankrupt	Medium	High	Critical	New supplier and installation company secured

Complete the risk management strategy for the project by listing each risk in full, making sure you accurately identify the project risks and apply the correct risk analysis methodology to the risk planning process.

Create a full and accurate risk plan with appropriate contingency plans that considers the relevant risks.

Think each risk through logically. Consider the risk itself, the probability or likelihood of the risk occurring in the project. The risk may be high, medium or low. Next, identify the likely impact on the business – high, medium or low. For example, if software is not compatible, alternative software may need to be sourced, in which case the impact on the business would be medium. Consider the severity of the risk occurring – catastrophic, critical, marginal, negligible. If the impact on the organisation of alternative software is medium, then the impact might be marginal. The Contingency Plan should identify possible actions to mitigate the risk.

Read the information carefully as you need to show that you have logically considered all of the relevant risks that show a full awareness of the given information.

Links Revise how to create a risk management strategy on page 117 of the Revision Guide.

Guided

Deliverables

Item	Components	Description
Online Training Booking System	Training event diary	Link to Trainer/Assessor and course diaries and invoice system

Complete the deliverables for the project by listing each one and its components and provide a detailed description.

 Links A deliverable is the actual outcome of the project or the product. To find out more about deliverables, see page 102 of the Revision Guide.

Project quality strategy

Guided

Stakeholders

Stakeholder	Responsibility
Managing Director	Project sponsor – provides the authority and guidance, and maintains the priority of the project in the organisation Control of finance
Project Manager	Responsible for defining, planning, controlling and leadership

List each of the stakeholders and their responsibilities for the project in full. Remember – a stakeholder is anyone interested in the success of the project. Consider internal and external stakeholders.

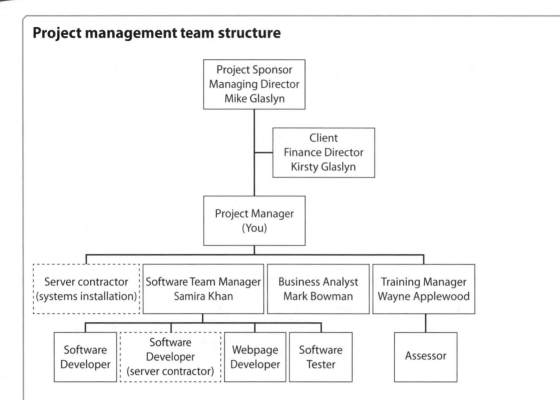

Project management team structure

Project Sponsor
Managing Director
Mike Glaslyn

Client
Finance Director
Kirsty Glaslyn

Project Manager
(You)

Server contractor
(systems installation)

Software Team Manager
Samira Khan

Business Analyst
Mark Bowman

Training Manager
Wayne Applewood

Software
Developer

Software
Developer
(server contractor)

Webpage
Developer

Software
Tester

Assessor

 Communication plan

Stakeholder(s)	Frequency	Type	Purpose
Managing Director	Weekly	Email informing them of the project status	Keep the Managing Director informed of progress to date

Complete the Communication plan for the project. Everyone involved in the project needs to be kept informed of the project status. List each of the internal key stakeholders accurately and the frequency of the communication, type of communication and the purpose of the communication.

Make sure you consider the most relevant communication methods and appropriate frequency of communication for the stakeholders to show that you are fully aware of the given scenario.

Accurately describe the purpose of all of the listed communications.

Links To revise how to put together a communication plan, see the Revision Guide, page 119.

Once you have completed the PID, check it carefully, then save it with the file name **revisionactivity1PID** as a word processed document and also as a PDF.

Revision activity 2

Project planning documentation is needed to go with your PID.

Produce the following documents based on the information provided in the scenario:

(a) a Gantt chart
(b) a resource list
(c) a cost plan.

(a) Produce a Gantt chart for the project.

Present your documents using appropriate software.

Days

Project stages	1	2	3	4	5	6	7	8	9	10	11	12	13	14	15	16	17	18	19	20	21	22	23	24	25	26	27	28	29	30	31
Start up																															
Analysis			◇																												
Design																															
Development																											◇				
Handover																															

You will need to use an appropriate software to create your Gantt chart.

Consider each of the following:

1. List the project stages/project sequences. Remember that some tasks may have to be completed before others or have dependencies.
2. Each end of stage should have a milestone.
3. Resources should be assigned to each task.

Make sure the Gantt chart shows project tasks in an efficient sequence for the scenario showing the final task completed by the given deadline.

Links You can revise how to complete a Gantt chart by looking at the Revision Guide, page 115.

Once completed, check your Gantt chart, then save it with the file name **revisionactivity2gantt** in the document's original file format and also as a PDF.

(b) Complete a resource list.

> Your list should include everything required to complete the project – hardware and software and human resources (the project team).

Guided

Resource list:	Staffing list:
Server hardware	Server contractor
Microsoft Windows server	Software Developer
Microsoft SQL server	....
....	....
....	....
....	....
....	....
....	....
....	....
....	....

> Once completed, check your resource list, then save it with the file name **revisionactivity2resource** in the document's original file format and also as a PDF.

(c) Complete a cost plan.

> From the scenario identify all of the project staff costs, hardware and software costs and other items that have a cost attributed to them.

> Some of the costs will have to be calculated for the period of the project as they may be given as an annual, daily or hourly rate.
>
> Make sure that all costs from the scenario are entered accurately, with all sections fully completed. You must produce an accurate estimate of the costs so that you can calculate whether the budget will be sufficient to cover the cost of the project.
>
> Use appropriate software to create your cost plan.

Guided

Cost plan

Training recording system budget	£80 000		
Hardware and software	**Amount**	**Item cost (£)**	**Total cost (£)**
Server hardware	1	2300	2300
Microsoft Windows server	1	2750	
Microsoft SQL server			
	4		
Total Hardware and software cost			

Using a spreadsheet, list all the hardware and software shown in your resource list. Insert the cost of each item from the figures provided in the information. Using an appropriate formula, calculate the total cost of the items. Remember, there may be multiple quantities of each item. Finally, calculate the total cost of hardware and software required for the project. You can use a calculator to help you if you wish.

Project team	Daily hrs	Hr cost (£)	5-days testing (£)	26 days (£)
Project Manager	6.5	50	1625	8450
Business Analyst				
Software Team Manager				
Software Developer				
Webpage Developer				
Total Project team costs				

Using your resource list, copy the staffing list (project team) into your spreadsheet.

Enter a formula to calculate the required costs for the 5-day testing and total costs.

Check your calculations are correct, using a calculator.

System installation	Daily hrs	Hr cost (£)	5-days testing (£)
System Installations costs	1	850	850
Server contractor Software Developer	1		
Components from another supplier	1		
Total System installations costs			

Your cost plan needs to include the total cost of the system installation.

Functional points	Daily hrs
Course Schedule module interface	5
Payment module	2
Trainer/Assessor module	
Venue module	
Client services	
Reporting module	
Total Functional points	

List all Functional points and calculate the total using an appropriate formula. Remember that all staff work 6.5 hours per day. The six modules comprise 19 functional points – allow for the additional costs of staff who require additional hours per functional point.

Use an appropriate formula to calculate the total cost for the daily rate and the duration of the project.

Additional costs per functional point	Daily hrs	FP	Hours	Cost (£)
Software Team Manager	2	19	38	1596
Software Developer	1	19	19	608
Webpage Developer	0.5	19	9.5	304
Software Tester	0.5	19	9.5	238
Total Additional costs per functional point				**2746**

The total equipment rental is also a pro-rata cost. Use an appropriate formula to calculate the total cost of the daily rate for the duration of the project.

Finally, use an appropriate formula to calculate the overall cost of the project, and whether it was under or over budget.

Equipment rental pro-rata cost	6.5-hour day (£)	Days	Costs (£)
Software Team Manager	24	31	744
Software Developer	19	31	589
Webpage Developer	24	31	
Software Tester	19	31	
Total Equipment rental pro-rata cost			

Total project cost		
Budget	£80 000	
Project under/over budget by	£	

Use appropriate software to create your cost plan.

Remember that all staff work 6.5 hours per day. The six modules comprise 19 functional points – allow for the additional costs of staff who require additional hours per function point.

 Links To revise Resources and budgeting look at the Revision Guide, page 116.

Once completed, check your cost plan, then save it with the file name **revisionactivity2cost** in the document's original file format and also as a PDF.

Revision task brief – part 2

The project is underway and you are monitoring and controlling its progress to its completion and closure.

You need to review the project's progress and lessons learned, taking into account the time and cost issues that have occurred, and communicate this information to the relevant members of the team using your company's Project Checkpoint Report document.

Information

The project has reached the point where the direct changeover of the Training Recording System is starting. However, there have been two issues to deal with during the system development stage

1. On 23 August, the Webpage Developer was still updating the Course Schedule database and the expected delay is 2 days. The Trainer/Assessor was asked to help the Webpage Developer update the Course Schedule database.

2. On 25 August, the server contractor had problems obtaining components for the computer and had to purchase the components from another supplier at an additional cost of £855.

Revision activity 3

Produce the Project Checkpoint Report for your project, using the document given. You will need to include information from the start of the project up to the end of the development stage, including:

- a summary of the work completed by the project team
- an issues log
- a summary of lessons learned.

You can access a template of a Project Checkpoint Report (PCR) for use in Revision task 1, Revision activity 3 by scanning this link with your smartphone or tablet and downloading the file called revisiontaskPCR.docx. Alternatively, go to the following link: http://activetea.ch/2xQQNzr and save the file on your laptop or computer ready for you to input information as you complete the revision activity.

Add further lines to the Project Checkpoint Report if required.

You may find it helpful to refer the project documentation you have already completed (PID, Gantt chart, resource list and cost plan) when producing your Project Checkpoint report.

Project Checkpoint Report

Report details

Date of checkpoint:	
Period covered:	End of User Testing

Version	Modifications	Author	Date
2	Webpage Developer's Course Schedule database update requires an additional 2 days. Gantt chart updated	Project Manager	23 August

The first approved version will be saved as version 1.

The 'Modifications' are a brief summary of changes carried out on the PCR.

The 'Author' of the document updated the document details.

The delay in updating the Course Schedule has been completed for you so you need to complete the PCR for the other issue.

Make sure that the information given in the brief is entered accurately with all sections fully completed.

Document approvals

This document requires the following approvals:

Name	Role	Signature	Date	Version
Mike Glaslyn	Managing Director	*Mike Glaslyn*	30 August	3

Complete each section in full and accurately.

The first name on the approval list has been completed for you – you need to complete the remaining name.

The project end date is the 31 August – look at your Gantt chart to identify when the direct changeover of the Training Recording System is scheduled to start.

Guided >

Document distribution

This document has been distributed to:

Name	Role	Date of Issue	Version
Mike Glaslyn	Managing Director	30 August	3

Guided >

Products

Product Name	Work Undertaken	Date Complete
Online training booking system	Testing of the online training booking system to ensure that it is free of errors	22 August

Make sure the product name given in the scenario is entered accurately and that the 'Work Undertaken' section is fully completed with the completion date. The first 'Product Name' has been completed for you so you need to complete the remaining Product Names.

Links To find out more about the Project Checkpoint Report see the Revision Guide, pages 135–136.

Guided >

Quality management

....

....

The Software Team Manager supported the Software Tester to use ISO/IEC 25010:2011 standard to test the new system.

....

Complete the Quality management section and Work package tolerance status for the project. In the Quality management section, list the activities undertaken during this period.

Make sure you enter the information accurately to show that you are fully aware of the scenario.

Links To revise Quality management, see the Revision Guide, page 118.

Work package tolerance status

Time	5 days
Cost	Staff costs approx. £
Quality	Testing

Identify a work package that occurred during the last stage of the project, the cost and any quality control processes. Calculate the cost, the scenario will provide the time period for the work package.

Links Have a look at the Work Breakdown Structure (WBS) on page 114 of the Revision Guide to find out more on work packages.

Issues log

Date Raised	Raised By	Description	Action Taken	Date Closed
23 August	Software Team Manager	The Webpage Developer is still updating the Course Schedule database. Expected delay is 2 days.	The Trainer/Assessor was asked to help the Webpage Developer update the Course Schedule database.	
	Finance Director			

Lessons learned:

Develop a system to ensure that the Course Schedule database is updated regularly.

....

....

Links To revise what is required at the project closure stage, see the Revision Guide, page 126.

Once completed, check your Project Checkpoint Report, then save it with the file name **revisionactivity3checkpoint** in the document's original file format and also as a PDF.

Reviewing the project

The project is complete.

The Software Team Manager and Training Manager reported that the direct changeover did not go well, the Course Training Schedule would not update.

The new system allowed the client to book the course online, but it did not send the invoice for the payment of the course to the client's email address and failed to link to the company accounts system.

The Finance Director has calculated that the final cost of the project was £77 434, just under the allocated budget of £80 000.

The Finance Director's concerns about the level of staff skills when using the new integrated system and the current hardware not being capable of processing all of the data did not materialise. The system was up and running on 1 September, although there were a few bugs on 31 August. Therefore, no contingency plan was required.

The Training Manager reported that the online system has allowed him to manage the course bookings better and he is able to see how many customers are attending the course. He can also plan for further courses as he can see the Trainer/Assessor's availability on the electronic diary.

Customer satisfaction has improved to 90 per cent – customers' records are accurate as they are updated by the customers themselves.

To close the project, you need to write a formal email to the project sponsor informing them of the following:

- how the project has performed against the three main success criteria
- an evaluation of how successful the project management has been throughout all stages of the project lifecycle
- a summary of all the lessons learned with an explanation of the key lessons that would be helpful to transfer to future projects, including successes as well as project issues.

You should now write to the project sponsor using your company's email document.

Revision activity 4

Produce your email to send to the project sponsor using your company's email document.

You can access a template of your company's email document for use in Revision task 1, Revision activity 4 by scanning this link with your smartphone or tablet and downloading the file called revisiontaskemail.docx. Alternatively, go to the following link: http://activetea.ch/2f8rG46 and save the file on your laptop or computer ready for you to input information as you complete the revision activity.

Remember to link your email to the scenario – refer to the documents you have produced throughout this revision task. Write clearly and concisely, using technical vocabulary where appropriate.
For each stage of the project, you could evaluate the costs, problems, achievements and if the stage was completed on time.

Email	
From	
To	Mike Glaslyn, Managing Director
Subject	Project close (Training Recording System)

Start up

> Start up – did the project start on time? Note the start-up date.

Analysis stage

> Analysis stage – who was involved, what was accomplished, any problems, completed on time?

Design stage

> Design stage – who was involved, what was accomplished, any problems, completed on time?

Development stage

> Development stage – completed on time? Provide an evaluation of the task undertaken.

User testing

> User testing – was this stage successful? Evaluate the success of the quality standard used. Completed on time? If not, explain why.

Installation

> Installation – was the installation carried out successfully by the contractor? Additional costs incurred? Evaluate the installation process.

Handover

> Handover – evaluate the outcomes of the project costs, resources, staff, risks, benefits of the project. Did the project achieve its objectives?

Lessons learned

> Lessons learned – what can be taken forward to new projects as best practice?

Conclusion

Conclusion – evaluate the overall success of the project. These are some of the points you will need to consider during the **evaluation**:

- All stages or milestones achieved
- Project staff release
- Deliverables/outputs tested and meet specification requirements
- Financial closure
- Lessons learned
- Sign off
- Documentation completed and archived.

 Links To revise Closing a live project and reviewing a project's success, see the Revision Guide, pages 126 and 127.

When you have finished writing your email, check it carefully, then save it with the file name **revisionactivity4email** in the document's original file format and also as a PDF.

Revision task 2

To support your revision, the task below helps you to revise the skills that you might need in your assessed task. The revision task consists of four activities based on a task brief. Electronic templates of a **Project Initiation Document**, **Project Checkpoint Report** and **Project Email** for use with the revision task (activities 1, 3 and 4) are available to download (see pages 68, 81 and 105 for information on how to access each of these).

The details of the actual assessed task may change, so always make sure you are up to date. Ask your tutor or check the Pearson website for the most up-to-date Sample Assessment Material to get an idea of the structure of your assessed task and what this requires of you.

Revision task brief – part 1

You are asked to use your project planning and management understanding and skills within a given computing project scenario.

You are the Project Manager in a sports equipment store, Fresh Sport Dynasty, that has an in-house team of a Business Analyst, Network Manager, Webpage Developer, Software Team Manager, Software Developers and a Software Tester. Your manager has allocated you to an in-house project to design and implement a new online ordering system and shopping service.

In the first part of the revision task, you will need to complete project documentation to initiate and launch a project to design and implement a new training recording system. In the second part of the task, you will monitor and control the project's progress to its completion and closure.

Read the information that follows. You will then use page 91 forward to make notes and complete Revision activity 1, and page 99 forward to make notes and complete Revision activity 2.

Information

The business case has been prepared by the Finance Director. The company has set aside £200 000 for the project.

It has been decided to implement the system using pilot changeover which will cover the sale of sports fitness equipment only.

The project timeline has been agreed. The start date will be 9 October and the pilot launch date will be 26 December to take advantage of Christmas store closure and the start of the January sales.

The principal role of the new online ordering system is to provide access to new markets, increase sales by 15 per cent within one year, reduce overheads by 10 per cent within six months and use customer intelligence to understand customer needs. The new online ordering system will also provide the business with a new stock control system that will, in turn, allow a comprehensive view of consumer purchases by products sales analysis ensuring that they can satisfy the customer needs better than the competition.

The current stock control system has become difficult to update. It does not provide any information on consumer purchases history and it cannot be used to analyse customer sales.

The Marketing Manager would also like a section on the website for customers to provide product reviews. It has been agreed that this will be scheduled for the next stage of the project.

The online ordering system will consist of a stock control database and must be linked to the company's website.

The new online system will incorporate a stock control database and has four modules:
- Orders online interface with business logic module (five functional points)
- Payment module (two functional points)
- Inventory and stock control management module (three functional points)
- Delivery management module (three functional points)

The Business Analyst will carry out the analysis of the current stock control and sales system on 9 October and create the requirements specifications. This is estimated to take two weeks.

The Business Manager and the Software Developer will start work on the system design on 23 October. Two weeks have been allocated to the project design stage.

The Software Team Manager has allocated a Software Developer, Webpage Developer and the Database Administrator to the project. It is estimated that the development of the new system will start on 5 November and will take four weeks.

The Database Administrator will be updating the ordering system and stock control database, during the system design stage of the project, in preparation for the company's new website and will work closely with the Webpage Developer who is currently working on another project. As he will be using World Wide Web Consortium (W3C®), he will be attending a World Wide Web Consortium (W3C®) course in preparation for the development.

The Quality Manager has allocated a Software Tester who is familiar with the requirements of ISO/IEC 25010:2011 standard to work on the project. The design, development and testing of the new system will be carried out using in-house expertise. The Acceptance testing stage will commence on 4 December and will last for two weeks.

The Finance Director has received tenders for the hardware and software. Although the cheapest tender was originally agreed, on 18 October the contractor informed the Finance Director that they were unable to install the equipment within the required timeframe. The Gantt chart was updated on 20 October to reflect the new date.

It was decided to purchase the new hardware and software from a local server contractor who will also install the new system at an additional cost. The server contractor has guaranteed that the hardware and software will be able to process the online sales website.

The Finance Director has agreed the hardware and software costs, these are:
- Server hardware £30 900
- Microsoft Windows server £39 495
- Microsoft SQL server £20 356
- Web development software £1900
- Microsoft Windows Azure £4100
- Microsoft Azure cloud storage £32 000

The server contractor has quoted for consultancy and installation costs of £39 500. The proposed installation date is 18 December. The installation will take one week. The server contractor has a full order book and requires at least two weeks' notification for delivery and installation. The hardware is guaranteed for six months.

The Finance Director is concerned about completing the project within budget and has asked the Project Manager to provide him with weekly expenditure reports. The Managing Director has also requested a copy of the weekly expenditure report and for all of the directors to be kept informed of the project progress through a daily email.

The Networking Service Director plans to install the latest version of the operating system, data is to be stored locally and backed up to cloud environment. The in-house network support team of two technicians and IT Help Desk technician support the IT services, but the director is concerned that they might not have the skills required to support the new system requirements. A specialist contractor is to be employed to install the new system but the system will be maintained using in-house technical expertise.

The Marketing Manager will act as the client for this project. He has identified two experienced members of staff from the sales team to help with the project, at no additional costs. The sales staff will send questionnaires to existing customers and work closely with the Business Manager and the company's Senior Software Developer during the analysis and design stage of the project, and then help with the acceptance testing for two weeks prior to the installation stage of the project.

The Finance Director has calculated the staff costs per hour for each person, to help with the project's budget planning:
- Project Manager £40
- Business Analyst £38
- Software Team Manager £39
- Software Developer £32
- Webpage Developer £32
- Database Administrator £32
- Software Tester £32

During the duration of the 11-week project all staff work a 5-day week, 6 hours per day.

The Finance Director has provided some additional cost information to help you plan the project.

Role	Hours per function point	Notes
Software Team Manager	3	Involved for the whole project
Software Developer	2	Involved for the whole project
Webpage Developer	2	Involved for the whole project
Database Administrator	2	Involved for the whole project
Software Tester	1	Involved for the whole project

Equipment rental	Pro-rata cost per week	Notes
Software Team Manager	£64	Full HD 24" LED High spec base unit
Software Developer	£32	21.5" LED Monitor
Webpage Developer	£32	21.5" LED Monitor
Database Administrator	£32	21.5" LED Monitor
Software Tester	£30	Laptop 19" screen

Company structure:

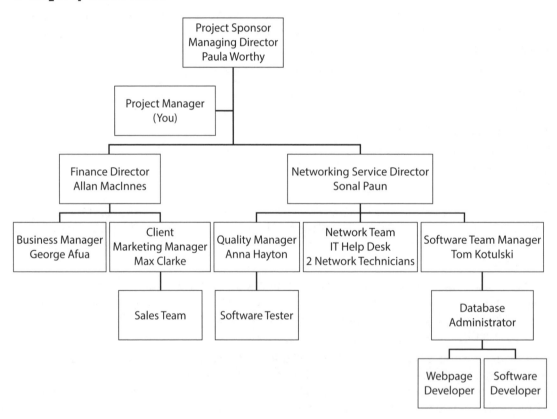

Revision task

The details of the actual set task may change so always make sure you are up to date. Ask your tutor or check the Pearson website for the most up-to-date Sample Assessment Material to get an idea of the structure of your set task and what this requires of you.

All the documents in this revision task should be produced using a computer. You will need to save your documents using the formats and naming conventions indicated.

Revision activity 1

Produce a Project Initiation Document for your project using the document provided.

You can access a template of a Project Initiation Document (PID) for use in Revision task 2, Revision activity 1 by scanning this link with your smartphone or tablet and downloading the file called revisiontaskPID2.docx. Alternatively, go to the following link: http://activetea.ch/2eQSCbU and save the file on your laptop or computer ready for you to input information as you complete the revision activity.

Add further lines to the Project Initiation Document sections if required.

The business case has already been populated. Option 1 (design and build a system using external skilled staff and subcontract support to an external computer system support company) has been chosen for this project.

Remember to take some time to read and understand the revision task brief, information and the tasks you are to complete. Make notes to use as you complete the project documentation.

Project Initiation Document

Project details

Project title	
Project Sponsor name	
Client name	
Project Manager name	
Start date	
Completion date	
Estimated cost	

Read the scenario carefully and make sure that the information from the scenario is entered accurately, with all sections fully completed.

Make sure that the dates are the same.

 Links For a reminder about the Project Initiation Document look at page 68.

Document details

Version	Modifications	Author	Date

All of the key stakeholders have to approve the updates.

Read the scenario carefully. Can you identify any changes, for example, cost, delivery, resources?

You should consider all of the project management documents to see if they have been updated.

Document approvals

Name	Role	Signature	Date	Version

The updated documents need to be distributed to all internal and external stakeholders.

Read the scenario carefully. You may have various versions of the PID that require approval.

All sections should be fully completed and the information entered should be relevant and accurate.

 Links For a reminder about who stakeholders are look at page 110 of the Revision Guide.

Document distribution

Name	Role	Date of Issue	Version

Purpose of the Project Initiation Document

Project aims:

....

....

....

....

....

....

....

....

> List the project aims from the scenario.
>
> Provide as much detail as you can. The information entered should be relevant to this project and accurate.

Project management and control:

....

....

....

....

> Think about the project management controls that are available to the Project Manager which relate to Resources, finance and the quality assurance process.

Links For a reminder about Quality assurance process look at page 102 of the Revision Guide.

Background to the proposed work

....

....

....

....

....

....

> The scenario will identify the reasons for the project so make sure you provide as much detailed and relevant information as possible.

Objectives

SMART Objective	Achieved?	Date and comments

Links For a reminder about writing SMART objectives look at page 103 of the Revision Guide.

Scope

....

....

....

....

....

....

....

....

....

....

> The scope must clearly define what the project will and will not cover and its limitations.
>
> All of the information you require will be in the scenario – internal and external influences, dates, resources and staff-related issues.

Business case

The current order processing system will not support the move into online sales.

There are two options:

1. Design, build and maintain our own system using in-house expertise.

2. Purchase a ready-made off the shelf product and subcontract support to an external networking company.

It has been agreed that option 1 is the preferred method.

The expected business benefit of the project is a measurable improvement in our order processing and improved sales through the online retail market. It is expected to:

- increase exposure to the online retail market to provide access to new markets
- increase sales by 15 per cent within one year
- reduce overheads by 10 per cent within six months and use customer intelligence to understand customer needs
- increase the number of orders handled from 15 per day to at least 30 per day within 3 months.

Timescale: the project should begin on 9 October with the pilot launch date of 26 December when the system will be implemented via pilot changeover for the sales of sports fitness equipment only.

The allocated budget for this project is £200 000 and the company expects a return of at least £7500 at the end of three years.

The major risks identified are:

- new technologies and processes used for the online sales website
- cost of hosting the new website
- increased stock purchasing costs and storage costs
- legal issues relating to security of customer details
- ongoing advertising costs
- in-house support of software and hardware
- staff development on new software and business processes, which may result in unforeseen problems, hold-ups and extra costs.

Assumptions

Assumption	Validated by	Status	Comments

Complete the assumptions for the project by listing each one, who validated it and comment on the status of the assumption.

An assumption is a low level risk that might happen or is required to deliver a successful project

Consider internal and external influences, resources, staff and quality standards.

 Links For a reminder about the difference between assumptions and constraints look at page 111 of the Revision Guide.

Constraints

Constraint	Validated by	Status	Comments

Complete the constraints for the project by listing each one, who validated it and its status. Provide detailed comments on the status of the constraint.

Consider internal and external influences, resources, staff and quality standards.

What is the status: catastrophic, critical, marginal or negligible?

 Links For help with Assumptions and constraints look at page 111 of the Revision Guide.

Risk management strategy

Risk	Probability	Impact	Severity	Contingency Plan

Complete the risk management strategy for the project by listing each risk in full, making sure you accurately identify the project risks and apply the correct risk analysis methodology to the risk planning process.

Create a full and accurate risk plan with appropriate contingency plans that considers the relevant risks.

Think each risk though logically. Consider the probability or likelihood of the risk occurring in the project – high, medium or low. Next, identify the likely impact (effect or disruption) on the business – high, medium or low.

Consider the severity of the risk occurring: catastrophic, critical, marginal, negligible.

The Contingency Plan should list possible actions taken to mitigate the risk.

Links You can revise how to complete the risk management strategy for the project on page 104 of the Revision Guide.

Deliverables

Item	Components	Description

Complete the deliverables for the project by listing each one and its components and provide a detailed description.

A deliverable is the actual outcome of the project or the product.

 Links For help with Quality and deliverables look at page 102 of the Revision Guide.

Project quality strategy

Stakeholders

Stakeholder	Responsibility

List each of the stakeholders and their responsibilities for the project in full.

Consider all stakeholders and their responsibilities.

🔗 **Links** For a reminder about Stakeholders look at page 110 of the Revision Guide.

Project management team structure

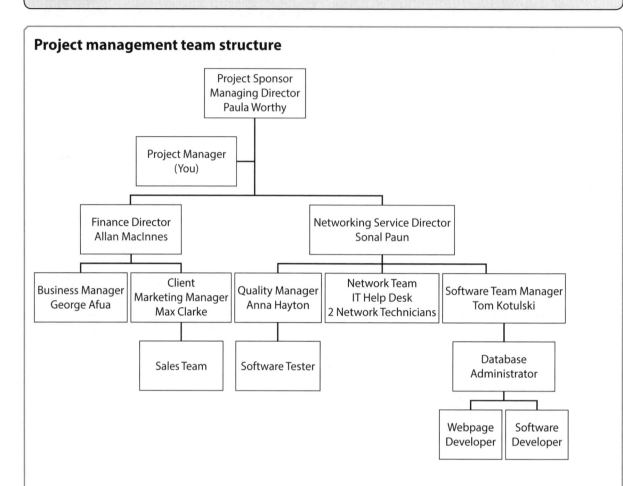

Communication plan

Stakeholder(s)	Frequency	Type	Purpose

Complete the communication plan for the project.

List each of the internal key stakeholders accurately and the frequency of the communication, type of communication and the purpose of the communication.

Identify the communication frequency, type and purpose of the communication.

🔗 **Links** Look at page 113 of the Revision Guide for help with completing a communication plan.

Once you have completed the PID, check it carefully, then save it with the file name **revisionactivity1PID** as a word processed document and also a PDF.

Revision activity 2

Project planning documentation is needed to go with your PID.

Produce the following documents based on the information provided in the scenario:

(a) a Gantt chart   (b) a resource list   (c) a cost plan.

Present your documents using appropriate software.

(a) Produce a Gantt chart for the project.

Days

Project stages	1	2	3	4	5	6	7	8	9	10	11	12	13	14	15	16	17	18	19	20	21	22	23	24	25	26	27	28	29	30	31
Start up																															
Analysis																															
System Design																															
System Development																															

Use appropriate software to create your Gantt chart.

Consider each of the following:

1. List the project stages/project sequences; some tasks may have to be completed before others or have dependencies.
2. Each end of stage should have a milestone
3. Resources should be assigned to each tasks.

Links You can revise how to complete a Gantt chart by looking at the Revision Guide, page 115.

Once completed, check your Gantt chart, then save it with the file name **revisionactivity2gantt** in the document's original file format and also as a PDF.

(b) Complete a resource list.

Resource list:	Staffing list:
....	....
....	....
....	....
....	....
....	....
....	....
....	
....	
....	
....	

Use appropriate software to create your resource list.

From the scenario identify all of the project staff, hardware and software costs and other items that have a cost attributed to them.

Use appropriate software to create your resource list.

From the scenario identify all of the project staff, hardware and software costs and other items that have a cost attributed to them.

(c) Complete a cost plan.

Use appropriate software to create your cost plan.

Add the costs to the resources list you have just created. Make sure it is accurate, with costs correctly attributed to provide an **accurate estimate** of the total project cost.

Remember that all of the staff work a 5-day week, 6 hours per day for the duration of the 11 week project.

The total number of functional points is 13.

 Links Look at page 116 of the Revision Guide for help with Resources and budgeting.

Once completed, check your cost plan, then save it with the file name **revisionactivity2cost** in the document's original file format and also as a PDF.

Revision task brief – part 2

To complete this part of the revision task, you will have completed Revision activities 1 and 2 on pages 91–100. You will need to refer to the documents that you have prepared.

For the actual assessment:
- The task information given will be different each year.
- Check with your tutor or look at the latest Sample Assessment Material on the Pearson website for details of how your task is structured and how the documents can be used.

The project is underway and you are monitoring and controlling its progress to its completion and closure.

You need to review the project's progress and lessons learned, taking into account the time and cost issues that have occurred, and communicate this information to the relevant members of the team using your company's Project Checkpoint Report document.

Information

The project has reached the acceptance testing stage of the system. However, there have been issues to deal with during the system development stage.

1. The Database Administrator is still updating the ordering system and stock control database. The expected delay is two weeks with a new end date of 15 December.
2. The World Wide Web Consortium (W3C®) course was postponed for one week. In addition, the Webpage Developer was delayed for one week on another project.

Revision activity 3

Produce the Project Checkpoint Report for your project, using the document given below. You will need to include information from the start of the project up to the end of the development stage, including:
- a summary of the work completed by the project team
- an issues log
- a summary of lessons learned.

You can access a template of a Project Checkpoint Report (PCR) for use in Revision task 1, Revision activity 3 by scanning this link with your smartphone or tablet and downloading the file called revisiontaskPCR.docx. Alternatively, go to the following link: http://activetea.ch/2xQQNzr and save the file on your laptop or computer ready for you to input information as you complete the revision activity.

Add further lines to the Project Checkpoint Report if required.

You may find it helpful to refer the project documentation you have already completed (PID, Gantt chart, resource list and cost plan) when producing your Project Checkpoint report.

Project Checkpoint Report

Report details

Date of checkpoint:	
Period covered:	

Version	Modifications	Author	Date

Read the scenario carefully and note any changes or problems in the project's progress.

The 'Modifications' should be a brief summary of changes carried out on the PCR.

The 'Author' of the document updated the document details.

Make sure that the information given in the scenario is entered accurately with all sections fully completed.

Document approvals

This document requires the following approvals:

Name	Role	Signature	Date	Version

The documents you completed for Activity 1 and Activity 2 will help you complete this task.

Complete each section accurately and in full.

The project end date is 26 December, the end of software development stage was week beginning 27 November.

Document distribution

This document has been distributed to:

Name	Role	Date of Issue	Version

Products

Product Name	Work Undertaken	Date Complete

Make sure the product name given in the scenario is entered accurately and that the work undertaken section is fully completed with the completion date.

 Links For help with Project Checkpoint Report look at pages 135 and 136 of the Revision Guide.

Quality management

....

....

....

In the Quality management section, list the activities undertaken during this period.

Make sure you enter the information accurately to show that you are fully aware of the scenario.

 Links Have a look at page 118 of the Revision Guide for a reminder about Quality management.

Work package tolerance status

Time	
Cost	
Quality	

Identify the time, cost and any quality control processes.

 Links Look at task scheduling and milestones on page 114 of the Revision Guide to find out more about work packages.

Issues log

Date Raised	Raised By	Description	Action Taken	Date Closed

Read the scenario carefully and see if you can find any issues.

Provide detailed information about the issue in each of the columns.

Lessons learned:

....

....

Make sure the lessons learned are relevant and show that you have a thorough understanding of project management concepts.

Consider:
• what went right
• what went wrong
• what could have been done better.

Once completed, check your Project Checkpoint Report, then save it with the file name **revisionactivity3checkpoint** in the document's original file format and also as a PDF.

Reviewing the project

The project was completed on 12 January.

The Networking Service Director reported that the pilot changeover went well and the new online sales website is fully functional.

The Finance Director has calculated the final cost of the project was £255 624 as all costs have been raised and paid.

The World Wide Web Consortium (W3C®) course was delayed for a week and the Web Developer was also delayed on another project.

The server developed a technical fault, and was replaced by the server contractor as guaranteed within the agreed six months' cover.

The Marketing Manager reported that the online system has allowed a comprehensive view of consumer purchases by products sales analysis ensuring that the company can satisfy customer needs.

During the analysis stage only 5 per cent of the questionnaires were returned. The sales staff carried out interviews for further market research which proved to be time consuming and costly and also the quality of responses varied by interviewer.

To close the project, you need to write a formal email to the project sponsor informing them of the following:

- how the project has performed against the three main success criteria
- an evaluation of how successful the project management has been throughout all stages of the project lifecycle
- a summary of all the lessons learned with an explanation of the key lessons that would be helpful to transfer to future projects, including successes as well as project issues.

You now need to write to the project sponsor using your company's email document.

Revision activity 4

Produce your email to send to the project sponsor using your company's email document.

> You can access a template of your company's email document for use in Revision task 1, Revision activity 4 by scanning this link with your smartphone or tablet and downloading the file called revisiontaskemail.docx. Alternatively, go to the following link: http://activetea.ch/2f8rG46 and save the file on your laptop or computer ready for you to input information as you complete the revision activity.

Email	
From	
To	
Subject	

Remember to link your email to the scenario – refer to the documents you have produced throughout this revision task. Write clearly and concisely, using technical vocabulary where appropriate.

Some of the points for you to consider during the evaluation:
- All stages or milestones achieved
- Project staff release
- Deliverables/outputs tested and meet specification requirements
- Financial closure
- Lessons learned
- Sign off
- Documentation completed and archived.

When reviewing project management, consider all aspects of the project lifecycle and try to make supported judgements about the issue or problem.

When you have finished writing your email, check it carefully, then save it with the file name **revisionactivity4email** in the document's original file format and also as a PDF.

Unit 4: Software Design and Development Project

Your set task

Unit 4 will be assessed through a task, which will be set by Pearson. You will need to use your skills and knowledge of software design, development, testing and evaluation to produce a program that meets a client's requirements.

Your Revision Workbook

This workbook is designed to **revise skills** that might be needed in your assessed task. The selected content, outcomes, questions and answers are provided to help you to revise content and ways of applying your skills. Ask your tutor or check the **Pearson website** for the most up-to-date **Sample Assessment Material** and **Mark Scheme** to get an idea of the structure of your assessed task and what this requires of you. Make sure you check the details in relation to completing work on a computer, the program languages that should be used, use of a data dictionary for the chosen language, use of a calculator, and any templates that may be provided. The details of the actual assessed task may change so always make sure you are up to date.

To support your revision, this workbook contains revision tasks to help you revise the skills that might be needed in your assessed task.

Your response to the tasks will help you to revise:

- producing a flow chart to plan the logic and processes for the program
- producing pseudocode that a software developer could use to create the program
- producing a test log to plan the testing of your complete program, including test data and expected result
- using your flow chart, pseudocode and test log to help write and test your program, which includes:
  - writing a program that meets the requirements of the task brief, in a C family or Python V3.4 or later version programming language
  - testing your solution to ensure that it functions as expected
  - recording the testing process in a test log and evaluation document.
- evaluating your program solution, by considering:
  - how well your solution meets the requirements of the scenario
  - the quality and performance of your program
  - the choices you made about coding conventions
  - the changes you made during the development process.
- writing your response in the evaluation section of a test log and evaluation document.

Links To help you revise skills that might be needed in your Unit 4 assessed task this workbook contains two revision tasks starting on pages 108 and 133. The first is guided and models good techniques, to help you develop your skills. The second gives you the opportunity to apply the skills you have developed. See the introduction on page iii for more information on features included to help you revise.

Revision task 1

To support your revision, the revision task below helps you revise the skills that might be needed in your assessed task. The revision task consists of five activities based on a task brief. An electronic template of a test log and evaluation document for use with the revision task (activities 3, 4 and 5) is available to download (see page 118 for information on how to access this).

The details of the actual assessed task may change so always make sure you are up to date. Ask your tutor or check the Pearson website for the most up-to-date Sample Assessment Material to get an idea of the structure of your assessed task and what this requires of you.

Revision task brief

You are asked to use your software design, development, testing and evaluation understanding and skills to produce a program that meets the client's requirements.

Read the information that follows on pages 108–111 and make notes. You will then use pages 112 forward to complete Revision activity 1, page 117 forward to complete Revision activity 2, page 118 forward to complete Revision activity 3, page 121 forward to complete Revision activity 4 and page 131 forward to complete Revision activity 5.

BrickBase, a popular trade supplier in the construction industry, is planning an experimental in-store purchasing system for its trade-only customers as a precursor to investing in a potentially expensive e-commerce version. You have been commissioned as the software developer who will write this trial program.

You need to create a program that provides the client with an efficient and robust solution.

You will design, implement and test your program. You will also need to justify and evaluate your decisions.

When designing and developing the solution, ensure you:

- read through the client interview and understand the nature of the problem and its scope
- produce a flow chart that:
  - uses British Computing Society symbols
  - identifies the required logic for the program
  - identifies the required processes for the program
- produce pseudocode that:
  - describes the tasks and processes needed to solve the problem
  - uses sequence, decisions and repetition appropriately
  - uses correct operations to solve tasks
  - uses hierarchy and indentation to highlight structure
  - demonstrates effective and efficient problem solving
- produce a test log that:
  - identifies the types of test which are required
  - identifies and categorises different choices of test data for each test
  - demonstrates expected results from your planned solution
- write your program using a language in the C family or Python V3.4 or later that:
  - demonstrates good design practices
  - includes techniques to improve code readability
  - creates and handles data correctly
  - performs arithmetic calculations accurately and reliably
  - uses built-in functions

- validates data input to ensure integrity
- uses appropriate control structures
- creates, populates and processes appropriate data structures
- update your test log by:
  - testing your program with the actual results of your planned tests
  - capturing screenshots of tests
  - analysing the testing outcomes and commenting upon them
  - using testing outcomes to refine accuracy, readability and robustness
- complete a written evaluation of your program that:
  - compares the software outcome against the requirements of the brief
  - identifies and describes the strengths of the software
  - identifies and describes the weaknesses of the software
  - identifies your learning and skill requirements from the process.

Information

You are provided with information to use when designing and developing your program:

- BrickBase – client interview
- BrickBase – in-store stock (sample)
- BrickBase – customer accounts (sample)
- BrickBase – invoice (sample).

BrickBase – client interview

'BrickBase currently has 20 stores across the UK and all stock is usually available at each store unless it needs reordering. Each stock item is identified by a simple 5-digit product code, has a short description and a price expressed in pounds and pence.

Our vision is for customers to be able to self-serve, adding products and quantities to their basket and, on checkout, generate the required invoices. Samples of our existing invoices are shown on page 112. Obviously we don't want customers to be able to buy products which aren't in stock so this should be checked.

In addition to their standard information, each customer has an associated discount which can vary depending on the credit terms they have with us and these vary between 5 per cent and 25 per cent. Unfortunately our account numbers vary in format so I can't give you a fixed format for these (they aren't always numeric). We would want an error to be displayed if the customer account number can't be found.

Most of our products are VAT (value added tax)-rated at 20 per cent, but there are some exceptions. For example, some items have a reduced VAT rate of 5 per cent and other items may actually be zero-rated if they are related to, for example, safety equipment. I have provided you with a small sample of BrickBase's in-store stock as shown on page 111 for testing purposes.

We would like all products stored in a data file which can be kept up to date to help manage stock levels for reordering per store – although we don't need you to add this functionality yet. Additionally, we feel that the system should operate using a simple menu system with options such as "1. enter customer account number", "2. add to basket", "3. checkout" and so on.

The program must work reliably and update stock levels when products are purchased, which will allow us to monitor stock levels more efficiently.'

Make sure you read the revision task brief thoroughly. Don't be tempted to go straight to the revision activities. Being clear on the task brief will ensure that you:
- fully understand what you have to do to satisfy the client's requirements
- identify the inputs, processes, storage and outputs required in the solution
- identify the data types, data structures and data-handling techniques and structures that you will need to use to form the solution
- use these to help you design a flow chart and the pseudocode that describes the solution.

Guided

1 What is the name of the business that forms the basis of the task?

....

2 Write down the six stages of the Software Development Life Cycle (SDLC), in order:

   (i)   Conception

   (ii) ....

   (iii) ....

   (iv) ....

   (v) ....

   (vi) ....

3 Write down your understanding of the trigger for this software development project.

BrickBase is planning an experimental in-store purchasing system for its trade-only

customers as a precursor to ....

....

....

....

....

The SDLC gives you a handy step-by-step framework for the activities you need to perform in order to solve BrickBase's problem satisfactorily.

Links For more on the SDLC, see the Revision Guide, page 139.

BrickBase's stock data will need to be stored in the program and in a data file. Think about which data types would be needed to store each value, for example, an account number with characters and digits would need to be stored as a string. For data files you need to think about the different formats of file which are available, for example, CSV (comma separated value), XML (eXtensible Markup Language) etc.

BrickBase – in-store stock (sample)

Product code	Description	Price ex VAT (£)	In Stock	Vat Rate (%)	Branch
10001	MDF board 2440 × 1220 × 18 mm	14.30	150	20	Lincoln
10002	Light MDF 2440 × 1220 × 18 mm	16.00	200	20	Lincoln
10003	MDF moisture resistant board 2440 × 1220 × 18 mm	27.60	120	20	Manchester
10005	MDF moisture resistant board 2440 × 1220 × 18 mm	27.60	80	20	Lincoln
10006	Plywood 2440 × 1220 × 18 mm	31	23	20	Bristol
10030	Red faced poplar 2440 × 1220 × 18 mm	12	44	20	Bristol
10031	Red faced poplar 2440 × 1220 × 18 mm	12	0	20	Lincoln
10045	Coveralls size XL	5.50	45	5	Bristol
10046	Condensing boiler safety manual	16.90	10	0	Bristol

BrickBase – customer accounts (sample)

Account Number	Account Name	Discount (%)	Shipping Address
DF123	A&B Plumbing	10	Withheld
56789	ConstructCo	7.5	Withheld
123765A	Pink Plumbers	5	Withheld
JONESBUILD	Roofing UK	0	Withheld

 Links For more on storing different types of data, see the Revision Guide page 12, Handling Data within a program, and page 182 Data structures.

Placing quotes around text entries is necessary if the text itself contains commas. Although this isn't the case with the BrickBase product data it is often considered good practice to do so, helping to distinguish text and numeric values.

4 CSV is perhaps the easiest file format that can store your product data accurately and is capable of being read by programs written in either Python 3.X or languages in the C family. Complete the following CSV file format for the BrickBase product data shown in the in-store stock table above.

"10001","MDF board 2440 × 1220 × 18 mm",14.30,150,20.0,"Lincoln"
"10002","Light MDF 2440 × 1220 × 18 mm",16.00,200,20.0,"Lincoln"
"10003","MDF moisture resistant board 2440 × 1220 × 18 mm",27.60,120,20.0,"Manchester"

....

....

....

....

....

....

The customer's invoice is the most important output from the program. Examine this to identify the results of calculations that need to be performed and output on screen. Also take note of labels and headings which you must display. This sample invoice can also give you some valuable test data if you want to use it, particularly in terms of expected results.

BrickBase – invoice (sample)

BRICKBASE INVOICE

Invoice for ConstructCo

Account number: 56789

Item	Description	Quantity	Price per item, excl VAT (£)	Sub-total incl. VAT (£)
10001	MDF board 2440 × 1220 × 18 mm	10	14.30	171.60
10002	Light MDF 2440 × 1220 × 18 mm	5	16.00	96.00
10003	MDF moisture resistant board 2440 × 1220 × 18 mm	4	27.60	132.48
Total				370.08
Saved				30.00

Revision task

The details of the actual set task may change, so always make sure you are up to date. Ask your tutor or check the Pearson website for the most up-to-date Sample Assessment Material to get an idea of the structure of your set task and what this requires of you.

All the documents in this revision task should be produced using a computer. You will need to save your documents using the formats and naming conventions indicated.

Revision activity 1

Produce a flow chart, using British Computing Society symbols, to plan the logic and processes for the program.

Before you start to draw the flow chart, think about the inputs, processes, storage and outputs required to satisfy the problem.

 Links You can remind yourself about inputs on pages 63 of the Revision Guide.

Inputs are values entered by the user (a BrickBase customer). They can include inputs used as part of navigating the program, such as a menu system, or for entering product codes and quantities. Think about what data the user needs to input in order for the processes to work and required outputs to be created.

 Guided

🖊 5 What inputs are required for this solution?

Customer menu option

Customer account number

....

....

....

....

Processes are usually linked with arithmetic calculations, checking user input, generating output etc. Examine the BrickBase client interview for a list of possible processes.

> **Guided** 🖎 6 What processes are required for this solution?

Validate product code

Check a product is in stock

....

Calculate cost of product added to basket

....

....

....

Calculate total invoice cost of order

....

....

....

There are two types of storage to think about – data stored in constants and variables, and the data you might want to store in a record (for a data file). Identifying variables is a good place to start as these will be linked to the inputs and outputs of the program. It is also helpful to start thinking about your data types, for example integers, strings etc.

> **Guided** 🖎 7 What data storage is required for this solution?

(a) Variables: Product code (string), Branch Name (string), ...

....

....

....

(b) Data file which stores stock data for each product: ....

....

....

Outputs can usually be thought of as the results of processes. Some outputs will be on-screen, others may be printed or written to a data file. You may also have existing documentation that will need to be generated by the program.

Guided

8 What outputs are required for this solution?

Customer menu options

....

Prompt for customer account

....

....

....

....

....

....

Links   For more on Flow charts see page 140 of the Revision Guide, which shows standard symbol conventions that you should follow to solve this task.

Think about the different menu options needed and then check which inputs, processes and actions are required for each branch of the menu. The next menu option to process would be option 2 – add to basket. Menu option 3 is similar but requires focusing on matching an inputted product code.

> Guided

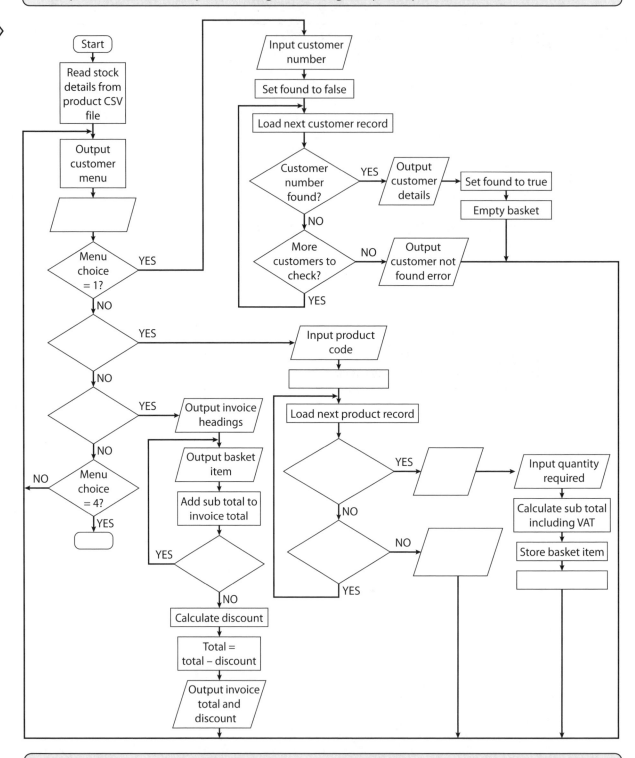

Save your flow chart as **revisionactivity1flowchart** in your chosen software format and also as a PDF.

Guided

Revision activity 2

Produce pseudocode that a software developer could use to create the program.

> **Links** Revise pseudocode on pages 9, 10 and 141 of the Revision Guide.

Complete the following pseudocode for this solution by filling in the statements, variables and values in the gaps shown. The flow chart you completed in Revision activity 1 should help you.

```
STORE customer accounts
    READ ........................................ from file
    REPEAT
      OUTPUT ..........................................
      INPUT ..........................................
      IF menu choice = 1 THEN
          INPUT ..........................................
          SET ..........................................
          REPEAT
            READ customer account
            IF customer account input = customer account number THEN
              OUTPUT customer information
              SET found = ..........................................
              SET discount %
            ENDIF
          UNTIL all customer accounts compared
          IF found = .......................................... THEN
            OUPUT "Customer not found" error message
          ENDIF
        ELSE
          IF menu choice = .............. THEN
            INPUT ..........................................
          SET found = false
          REPEAT
            READ stock detail
            IF product code = stock detail product code THEN
              OUTPUT stock details
              INPUT ..........................................
              Add stock details and quantity required to basket
              Subtotal = product price X ..........................................
              SET found = true
            ENDIF
          UNTIL all stock details compared
          IF found = false THEN
            OUTPUT "..........................................." error message
        ENDIF
```

```
        ELSE
          IF menu choice = .............. THEN
            OUTPUT Invoice header
            FOR 1 to basket items
              total = total + ...........................................
              OUTPUT ...........................................
            ENDFOR
            total = total − ...........................................
            OUTPUT total
            Empty basket
          ENDIF
        ENDIF
      ENDIF
    UNTIL ........................................... = .............. (exit)
```

Save your pseudocode as **activity2pseudocode** in your chosen software format and also as a PDF.

Revision activity 3

Produce a test log to plan the testing of your complete program, including test data and expected result.

Show your test planning by completing the test log section of the test log and evaluation document (see page 119).

You can access a template of the test log and evaluation document for use in Revision activity 3 by scanning this link with your smartphone or tablet and downloading the file called testlogandevaluation.docx. Alternatively, go to the following link: http://activetea.ch/2f7thaj and save the file on your laptop or computer ready for you to input information as you complete Revision activities 3–5.

 Links For more information on Test data, see page 142 of the Revision Guide.

For the Revision task, you will need to complete a test log and evaluation document, as shown below.

- Columns 1–4 of the test log are to be completed in Revision activity 3.
- Columns 5 and 6 (shown in grey) are to be completed in Revision activity 4 following testing of your program.
- The software evaluation section is to be completed in Revision activity 5.

A template of the test log and evaluation document is available to download (see page 118 for details of how to do this).

The details of the actual set task may change so always make sure you are up to date. Ask your tutor or check the Pearson website for the most up-to-date Sample Assessment Material to get an idea of the structure of your set task and what this requires of you.

Test log and evaluation

Add additional rows and extend the evaluation space as required.

Program language the product is to be produced in (tick box):

Python ☐   C Family ☐

Test number	Purpose of test	Test data	Expected result	Actual result	Comments
Software evaluation					

9 When you are testing the functionality, stability and usability of a solution there are three different types of test data you should consider.

Fill in the gaps in the test data selection table below. First identify the three types of test data.

Types of test data	1..........................	2..........................	3..........................
Menu option	1		X
Customer account number	DF123		
		10078	
Quantity required		1000	ABC

Fill in the gaps in the test log by identifying each test and its selected test data. Trace the flow chart (Revision activity 1) and/or pseudocode (Revision activity 2) to determine an expected result.

Test log

Test number	Purpose of test	Test data	Expected result	Actual result	Comments
1	Menu option 1 chosen	1	User asked for account number		
2	Invalid (normal) account number input		Outputs "Customer not found" error message		
3	Valid account number input	DF123			
4	Menu option 2 chosen	2			
5	Invalid (normal) product code input		"Product code not found" error message		
6	Valid (normal) product code input		Stock details shown and user asked for quantity		
7	Valid (extreme) quantity input		Outputs "invalid quantity" error message		
8	Invalid quantity input	ABC			
9	Valid quantity input				
10	Menu option 3 chosen				
11	Menu option 5 chosen (extreme)				
12	Menu option X chosen (invalid)				
13	Menu option 4 chosen				

You are unable to complete the 'Actual Result' and 'Comments' columns until the program code has been written and successfully run – see Revision activity 4. It is only then that you can capture actual screen output and compare these to your expected results. Leave these columns blank for now.

Once you have completed your test log and evaluation document, save the file as **revisionactivity3testlog** in your chosen software format and also as a PDF.

Revision activity 4

Write and test your program. Use your flow chart, pseudocode and test log to help you.

Part 1: Write the program

The solution can be solved in either a C family language or Python V3.4 or later version programming language. It is possible to develop working designs (flow charts, pseudocode) into either programming language. However, each language has its own particular syntax and layout which you need to be confident with before starting this task. Areas to revise before progressing include handling data, arithmetic options, functions, validation, control structures and data structures.

Links You can find detailed examples of both C family and Python programming language components throughout pages 146 to 149 of the Revision Guide. In addition you should also think about issues related to Code readability as described on page 145 of the Revision guide.

Choose EITHER the C++ solution OR the Python solution below, and fill in the missing sections.

Once you have completed the revision task, you could try filling in the other solution for further practice.

Sample C++ solution

> This section of code declares the various data structures used by the C++ version of the program.

Guided   (a) Complete the missing sections which specify the data types for members of the following data structures used by the solution.

```cpp
#include <iostream>
#include <fstream>
#include <string>
#include <iomanip>

using namespace std;

//function prototypes
void outputCustomerMenu(void);
int readStockDetails(void);

//customer account structure
struct customerAccount {
                    accountNumber;
                    accountName;
                    discountPercentage;
                    shippingAddress;
};

//product structure
struct productDetail {
                    productCode;
                    productDescription;
                    productPrice;
                    inStock;
                    vatPercentage;
                    branch;
};

//basket detail
struct basketDetail {
    int productPosition;
    int quantity;
    float subTotal;
};
```

> This section of code declares constants, data structures and the main variables used by the C++ version of the program.

(b) In the solution below, complete the missing sections which specify the values of the customer accounts, the size of the arrays used to store the basket items and the products stored and the data types and comments of various local declarations.

```
//constants
const int MAXBASKET = 10;

const int MAXPRODUCTS = [        ] ;
```

This section of code handles the first two menu options of the C++ version of the program.

```
//customer account records
customerAccount Accounts[4] = { { "DF123","A&B Plumbing",10.0f,"Withheld" },
                                {                                          },
                                {                                          },
                                {                                          } };
```

```
//products
productDetail Products[        ];
```

```
//basket items
basketDetail BasketItems[        ];
```

```
int main() {

    //local declarations

    [        ] menuChoice;              //menu choice input by user
             productCode;               //product code input by user
             customerNumber;            //customer account number input by user
             quantityRequired;          //quantity of product input by user
             found;                     //whether customer or product found
             subTotal;                  //sub total value of items purchased
             total;                     //total value of items purchased
             activeDiscount;

    basketDetail newBasketItem;
    productDetail singleProduct;
    int basketItemCount;
    int customerPosition;
    int productsLoaded;



    //intialisations

    subTotal = 0.0f;
    total = 0.0f;
    activeDiscount = 0.0f;
    basketItemCount = 0;
    customerPosition = 0;
    quantityRequired = 0;
```

(c) Complete the missing sections of this solution.

```cpp
//load the products from file
productsLoaded = readStockDetails();

do {




    cin >> menuChoice;
    if (menuChoice == 1) {
        cout << "\nPlease enter customer number: ";
        cin.ignore();
        getline(cin, customerNumber);
        found = false;

        for (int counter=0;counter<sizeof(Accounts)/sizeof(*Accounts);counter++){
            if (customerNumber == Accounts[counter].accountNumber) {
                cout <<"\n\nCustomer Details found:" << endl;
                cout <<"Account: " << Accounts[counter].accountNumber << endl;




                found = true;
                activeDiscount = Accounts[counter].discountPercentage;
                basketItemCount = 0;
                customerPosition = counter;
            }
        }
        if (!found) {
            cout << "Sorry, account \'"<<customerNumber<<"\' was not found."<<endl;
        }
    }
    else {
        if (menuChoice == 2) {
            cout << "\nPlease enter product code: ";
            cin.ignore();
            getline(cin, productCode);
            found = false;
            for (int counter = 0; counter < productsLoaded; counter++) {
                if (productCode == Products[counter].productCode) {
                    cout <<"\n\nProduct found:" << endl;
                    cout <<»Product code: «<<Products[counter].productCode << endl;
                    cout <<»Description: «<<
                    cout <<»Price ex. VAT: £"<<
                    cout << "Vat Rate: "<<
                    cout << "Branch: " <<
                    cout << "Please enter quantity required: ";
                    cin >> quantityRequired;
                    subTotal = quantityRequired * Products[found].productPrice * <...>
                    (1 + Products[found].vatPercentage / 100);
                    newBasketItem.productPosition = counter;
                    newBasketItem.quantity = quantityRequired;
                    newBasketItem.subTotal = subTotal;
                    BasketItems[basketItemCount++] = newBasketItem;
                    found = true;
                }
            }
            if (!found) {




            }
        }
    }
```

> This section of C++ code outputs the customer's invoice and describes the function which displays the main menu.

(d) Complete the missing sections of this solution.

```
        else {
            if (menuChoice == 3) {

                                                                    
                                                                    
                                                                    

                cout <<"\nInvoice for"<<Accounts[customerPosition].accountName<<endl;
                cout << "Account number : " <<Accounts[customerPosition].<…>
                accountNumber<<endl;
                cout << endl << setw(8) << "Item" << setw(50) << "Description" << <…>
                setw(10);
                cout << "Quantity" << setw(8) << "Price" << setw(10) << "Sub-total" <…>
                << endl;
                for (int counter = 0; counter < basketItemCount; counter++) {
                    total = total + BasketItems[counter].subTotal;
                    singleProduct = Products[BasketItems[counter].productPosition];
                    cout << setw(8) << singleProduct.productCode;

                                                                    
                                                                    
                                                                    
                                                                    
                                                                    
                                                                    
                                                                    

                }
                customerDiscount= (total/100*Accounts[customerPosition].<…>
                discountPercentage);
                total = total - customerDiscount;
                cout << endl << setw(76) << "Total = £" << setw(10) << total << endl;
                cout << setw(76) << "Saved = £" << setw(10) << customerDiscount << endl;
            }
        }
    }

} while (menuChoice!= 4);

return 0;
}



/*
 * function to display customer menu options
 *
 */
void outputCustomerMenu(void) {
    cout << "\n\n------------" << endl;
    cout << "Customer Menu" << endl;
    cout << "------------" << endl;

                                                                    
                                                                    
                                                                    
                                                                    
                                                                    

    cout << "\nPlease enter your choice (1-4): ";
}
```

This section of code declares the various data structures used by the C++ version of the program.

```
/*
 * function to read stock details from CSV file and
 * store in as an array of products
 *
 * returns the number of products read from CSV file.
 */
int readStockDetails(void) {
        ifstream productFile;
        int productLine;
        string tempString;

        productLine = 0;
        productFile.open("products.csv");
        while (!productFile.eof()) {
            //get product code and remove quotes
            getline(productFile, Products[productLine].productCode, ',');
            Products[productLine].productCode.erase(0,1);
            Products[productLine].productCode.erase(Products[productLine]. <…>
            productCode.size()-1);

            //get product description and remove quotes
            getline(productFile, Products[productLine].productDescription, ',');
            Products[productLine].productDescription.erase(0, 1);

            Products[productLine].productDescription.erase(Products[productLine].
            productDescription.size() -  1);

            //get product price and convert to float
            getline(productFile, tempString, ',');
            Products[productLine].productPrice = ::atof(tempString.c_str());

            //get in stock and convert to float

            ┌----------------------------------------------------------┐
            ¦                                                          ¦
            └----------------------------------------------------------┘

            //get VAT rate and convert to float
            getline(productFile, tempString, ',');
            Products[productLine].vatPercentage = ::atof(tempString.c_str());

            //get branch and remove quotes

            ┌----------------------------------------------------------┐
            ¦                                                          ¦
            ¦                                                          ¦
            ¦                                                          ¦
            └----------------------------------------------------------┘

            //next product
            productLine++;
        }
        productFile.close();
        return --productLine;
}
```

Sample Python solution

(a) Complete the missing sections in this solution.

```python
import csv

#function to read stock details from CSV file
def readStockDetails():
  productFile = open('products.csv','r')
  reader = csv.reader(productFile)
  for eachProduct in reader:
    Products.append(eachProduct)
  productFile.close()

#function to display customer menu options
def outputCustomerMenu():
  print('-------------')
  print('Customer Menu')
  print('-------------')

```

```python

#customer account record
Accounts = {1: {'accountNumber': 'DF123', 'accountName': 'A&B Plumbing', <…>
'discountPercentage' :10.0, 'shippingAddress': 'Withheld'},

```

```python
}

#products
Products = []

#basket items
BasketItems = [[] for _ in range(    )]

newBasketItem = [0,0,0]
singleProduct = []

#intitialisations
activeDiscount = 0
basketItemCount = 0
customerPosition = 0
quantityRequired = 0
total = 0

#load the products from file

while True:
    outputCustomerMenu()


    menuChoice = int(input())
    found = False
```

```
if (menuChoice == 1):
  customerNumber = input('Please enter customer number: ')
  for eachAccount, value in Accounts.items():
    if customerNumber == value['accountNumber']:
      print('Customer Details found:')
      print('Account: ', value['accountNumber'])




      found = True;
      activeDiscount = value['discountPercentage']
      basketItemCount = 0
      total = 0
```

(b)

```
        customerPosition = eachAccount
    if (not found):
      print('Sorry, account, "', customerNumber, '" was not found.')
  else:
    if (menuChoice == 2):
      productCode = input('Please enter product code: ')
      found = False
      for index, eachProduct in enumerate(Products):
        if productCode == eachProduct[0]:
          print('Product found:')
          print('Product code: ', eachProduct[0])

          ┌─────────────────────────────────────────────────────────┐
          │                                                         │
          │                                                         │
          │                                                         │
          │                                                         │
          └─────────────────────────────────────────────────────────┘

          quantityRequired = int(input('Please enter quantity required: '))
          subTotal = quantityRequired * float(eachProduct[2]) * <...>
          (1+float(eachProduct[4])/100)
          newBasketItem = [index, quantityRequired, subTotal]
          BasketItems[basketItemCount] = newBasketItem
          basketItemCount = basketItemCount + 1
          found = True;

      if (not found):
          ┌─────────────────────────────────────────────────────────┐
          │                                                         │
          │                                                         │
          └─────────────────────────────────────────────────────────┘

    else:
      if (menuChoice == 3):
        print ('BRICKBASE INVOICE')
        print ('----------------')
          ┌─────────────────────────────────────────────────────────┐
          │                                                         │
          │                                                         │
          │                                                         │
          └─────────────────────────────────────────────────────────┘
        print ('{:>8}'.format('Item'),'{:>50}'.format('Description'),end='')
        print ('{:>10}'.format('Quantity'),'{:>8}'.format('Price'),end='')
        print ('{:>10}'.format('Sub-total'))
        for counter in range (0, basketItemCount):
          total = total + BasketItems[counter][2]
          singleProduct = Products[BasketItems[counter][0]]
          print('{:>8}'.format(singleProduct[0]),end='')

          ┌─────────────────────────────────────────────────────────┐
          │                                                         │
          │                                                         │
          │                                                         │
          └─────────────────────────────────────────────────────────┘

        customerDiscount = (total /100 * Accounts[customerPosition]['discountPercentage'])
        total = total - customerDiscount
        print ('{:>76}'.format('Total = £'), '{:>10}'.format(total))
        print ('{:>76}'.format('Saved = £'), '{:>10}'.format(customerDiscount))

      else:
        if (menuChoice == 4):
          break;
```

Once you have written your program, save your code as **revisionactivity4code** as a .txt file and also as a PDF.

Part 2: Test your solution

In Revision activity 3, you filled in the first part of the test log. Now you will need to test your solution, and complete the log with the actual result and any comments. Use screen captures to show the result of each test. If the program crashes or behaves unexpectedly, make a note in the comments column.

> **Guided**   **Test log**

Test number	Actual result	Comments
1	``` - - - - - - - Customer Menu - - - - - - 1. Login customer 2. Add products to basket 3. Checkout 4. Exit Please enter your choice (1-4): 1 Please enter your customer number: _ ```	Program works as expected
2		
3		
4		
5		
6		
7		
8		
9		
10		
11		
12		
13		

Once you have completed the test log with your results, save your test log and evaluation document as **revisionactivity4log** in your chosen software format and also as a PDF.

Revision activity 5

Evaluate your program solution. Write your response in the evaluation section of your test log and evaluation document.

> Your evaluation should cover:
> - how well your solution meets the requirements of the revision task brief
> - the quality and performance of your program
> - the choices you made about coding conventions
> - the changes you made during the development process.

> Your evaluation needs to review the design, the testing and the software solution produced. You will find guidance on this from pages 169 to 171 of the Revision Guide.

> Guided

Software Evaluation:

Evaluation of the design

The design has covered the basic specification as described by the client. The flow chart uses

the BCS symbols correctly and presents a workable solution. The pseudocode ....

....

....

....

One aspect of the design has been missed. This is the ....

....

....

....

....

....

....

Evaluation of the software testing

The test plan has identified the major inputs for the solution and attempts have been made to

test a range of data. However, testing could be improved by ....

....

....

....

....

....

....

....

Evaluation of the software

The coding has been written using a range of program language components and, generally, has meaningful identifier names and uses indentation consistently to highlight the structure and logic of the solution. The products are successfully read from a CSV data file using a separate function. During testing the program worked reliably and produced accurate results in an efficient manner.

Data types and structures are ....

....

....

....

Functions have ....

....

....

....

....

The solution is incomplete and does not fully meet the needs of the client. In particular, ...

....

....

....

....

....

....

....

> Once you have completed your evaluation, save the test log and evaluation document as **revisionactivity5evaluation** in your chosen software format and also as a PDF.

Revision task 2

Revision task brief

You are asked to use your software design, development, testing and evaluation understanding and skills to produce a program that meets the client's requirements.

Read the information that follows on pages 133–135. Take time to make sure that you understand the information before starting the activities. Then complete Revision activities 1–5 on pages 136–137.

Manor Road Primary School has 400 pupils studying at Key Stage 2. Due to recent concerns about online safety, the head teacher has contacted your company to build a simple computerised multiple-choice question and answer (MCQA) system. This will be used offline and loaded with different subjects. You have been commissioned as the software developer who will design and code this program.

You need to create a program that provides the client with an efficient and robust solution.

You will design, implement and test your program. You will also need to justify and evaluate your decisions.

When designing and developing the solution, ensure you:

- read through the client interview and understand the nature of the problem and its scope
- produce a flow chart that:
  - uses British Computing Society symbols
  - identifies the required logic for the program
  - identifies the required processes for the program
- produce pseudocode that:
  - describes the tasks and processes needed to solve the problem
  - uses sequence, decisions and repetition appropriately
  - uses correct operations to solve tasks
  - uses hierarchy and indentation to highlight structure
  - demonstrates effective and efficient problem solving
- produce a test log that:
  - identifies the types of test which are required
  - identifies and categorises different choices of test data for each test
  - demonstrates expected results from your planned solution
- write your program using a language in the C family or Python V3.4 or later that:
  - demonstrates good design practices
  - includes techniques to improve code readability
  - creates and handles data correctly
  - performs arithmetic calculations accurately and reliably
  - uses built-in functions
  - validates data input to ensure integrity
  - uses appropriate control structures
  - creates, populates and processes appropriate data structures

- update your test log by:
  - testing your program with the actual results of your planned tests
  - capturing screenshots of tests
  - analysing the testing outcomes and commenting upon them
  - using testing outcomes to refine the accuracy, readability and robustness
- complete a written evaluation of your program that:
  - compares the software outcome against the requirements of the brief
  - identifies and describes the strengths of the software
  - identifies and describes the weaknesses of the software
  - identifies your learning and skill requirements from the process.

Information

You are provided with information to use when designing and developing your program:

- Manor Road Primary School – client interview (with Head Teacher)
- Manor Road Primary School – subjects required
- Manor Road Primary School – sample subject questions and answers
- Manor Road Primary School – MCQA desired layouts

Manor Road Primary School – client interview (with Head Teacher)

'We try and ensure our learners are both IT literate and online safety conscious before they move to secondary school. Although our learners have supervised access to the internet and the PCs are protected against undesirable web sites and content, there are still instances which we'd like to protect against, for example, blocking some adverts and images.

One suggestion made at a staff meeting was to create a standalone program that allows learners to select different subjects and presents them with simple interactive multiple-choice question and answers (MCQA).

Once the program has been written, we would like to be able to expand the number of subjects and create new questions and answers, either through simple modification of the program's code or by loading questions onto a spreadsheet and exporting them into a program-friendly format.

Unfortunately, my technical background is centred on databases and computer graphics and the only programming I have done is with simple app builders – this is beyond my current skillset to complete. However, I am learning Python and C++ in my spare time in anticipation of being able to maintain it in the future so, if possible, these are the languages I would like the program to be written in.

To give you a head start I have included the list of subjects we'd like pre-loaded and some sample questions and answers for each. I have also attempted a rough sketch of how I'd like the program to look on screen. This includes a post-quiz breakdown of each question showing the pupil whether they got the question correct and if not, the correct answer.

We had also considered including a high-score table where pupils could enter their name so that there is a competitive element. I haven't sketched that but I'm sure you know the type of thing I mean; I'll leave the design of that to you.'

Manor Road Primary School – subjects required)

Geography	20 questions covering topics such as flags, capital cities, continents, oceans, mountains
Science	5 questions covering basic scientific principles, e.g. electricity, planets, chemicals, basic biology and botany
Mathematics	10 questions covering topics such as basic formulae, decimals, fractions and percentages

Manor Road Primary School – sample questions and answers

Geography	Question 1
	Which country's flag is white with a red disc?
	   A. China
	   B. Japan
	   C. India
	   D. USA
	Answer: B

Science	Question 1
	Which word is used to describe something that is dog-like?
	   A. Feline
	   B. Piscine
	   C. Canine
	   D. Porcine
	Answer: C

Mathematics	Question 1
	Which fraction is the largest?
	   A. 1/2
	   B. 2/3
	   C. 3/4
	   D. 2/4
	Answer: C

Manor Road Primary School – MCQA desired layouts

Manor Road Primary School
Subject Quiz

Subject: Maths (10 questions available)

Question 1

Which fraction is the largest?

   A. 1/2
   B. 2/3
   C. 3/4
   D. 2/4

Input your choice: ☐

Manor Road Primary School

Subject Quiz – answers

Subject: Maths (10 questions available)

Question 1: Correct (C)

Question 2: Correct (B)

Question 3: Incorrect, the correct answer is: B – 0.25

Etc

You scored 8 out of 10.

Revision task

The details of the actual set task may change, so always make sure you are up to date. Ask your tutor or check the Pearson website for the most up-to-date Sample Assessment Material to get an idea of the structure of your set task and what this requires of you.

All the documents in this revision task should be produced using a computer. You will need to save your documents using the formats and naming conventions indicated.

Revision activity 1

Produce a flow chart, using British Computing Society symbols, to plan the logic and processes for the program.

This solution must load questions from a file. Each filename is essentially the school subject, so it is probably a good idea to display a menu of the available school subjects for the learner to choose from. When an option is chosen, the correct file of questions should be loaded. Each question needs to be shown in turn, giving the learner a chance to select the correct answer. A simple decision could be used to compare the learner's answer with the correct answer to see if they are right. A simple counter can be used to keep track of their score. Various data structures could be used to maintain a high-score table and it should be sufficient to identify a sorting library (in-built) function, leaving the detailed implementation to the target programming language for now.

Save your flow chart as **revisionactivity1flowchart** in your chosen software format and also as a PDF.

Revision activity 2

Produce pseudocode that a software developer could use to create the program.

Save your pseudocode as **activity2pseudocode** in your chosen software format and also as a PDF.

Revision activity 3

Produce a test log to plan the testing of your complete program, including test data and expected result.

Show your test planning by completing the test log section of the test log and evaluation document (see page 119).

You can access a template of the test log and evaluation document for use in Revision activity 3 by scanning this link with your smartphone or tablet and downloading the file called testlogandevaluation.docx. Alternatively, go to the following link: http://activetea.ch/2f7thaj and save the file on your laptop or computer ready for you to input information as you complete Revision activities 3–5.

Testing for this program solution involves following a learner's use of the program, for example, selecting a particular subject, answering questions (correct, incorrect and using invalid options) and observing the responses received. You should check that the scores are reset between different runs and that answers are correctly identified as being correct or incorrect.

Once you have completed your test log and evaluation document, save the file as **revisionactivity3testlog** in your chosen software format and also as a PDF.

Revision activity 4

Write and test your program. Use your flow chart, pseudocode and test log to help write and test your program.

Remember to make sure that your program meets the requirements of the revision task brief. Write your program in a C family or Python V3.4 or later version programming language. Test your solution to ensure that it functions as expected and record the actual testing in your test log and evaluation document.

Both Python and C family languages have various data structures which could be used to solve this problem. In addition, both have built-in functions to process data files and sort the high-score table. Data structures such as arrays, lists and dictionaries are likely to be used in this solution.

Once you have written your program, save your code as **revisionactivity4code** as a .txt file and also as a PDF.

Once you have completed the test log with your results, save your test log and evaluation document as **revisionactivity4log** in your chosen software format and also as a PDF.

Revision activity 5

Evaluate your program solution. Write your response in the evaluation section of your test log and evaluation document.

Remember to cover:
- how well your solution meets the requirements of the revision task brief
- the quality and performance of your program
- the choices you made about coding conventions
- the changes you made during the development process.

Remember that your evaluation needs to review the design, the testing and the software solution produced.

Once you have completed your evaluation, save the test log and evaluation document as **revisionactivity5evaluation** in your chosen software format and also as a PDF.

Answers

Unit 1: Principles of Computer Science

Answers to Revision test 1

1 (a) Your answer should include any three of the following:
- Taxi sprite X coordinate
- Taxi sprite Y coordinate
- Amount of money
- Current status of a square

(b) Method: £65 + (£25 + £20 + £15 + £12 + £28 + £13) − £50
= £65 + 113 − £50
Answer: £128

(c)
```
BEGIN
IF key held down
        Increase speed
IF NOT touching wall
        Move right
        If touching square
                If square colour is white
                        Apply positive outcome
                If square colour is black
                        Apply negative outcome
END
```

(d)
- Code responding to the Ctrl key is duplicated in lines 6–14, 18–26, 30–38, 42–50, this code is only needed once at the start of the subroutine.
- The duplicated code responding to the Ctrl key in lines 6–14, 18–26, 30–38, 42–50, can be greatly simplified by using an IF structure to add 2 to the variable, MoveDistance, if it holds 4 or less.

(e)
- The duplicated code responding to the Ctrl key in lines 6–14, 18–26, 30–38, 42–50, is flawed as it cannot reduce MoveDistance, the code needs to respond to an arrow key used which is opposite to the direction currently travelled.
- Use of MoveDistance as a global variable is probably inappropriate but it is difficult to be sure from the code here. If MoveDistance is to be used only in the subroutine shown, better practice would be to declare it as a static variable, so private to the subroutine and also retaining value from the last time the subroutine ran.

(f) Your answer should include **one** point for each symbol:
Decision
- Ctrl key pressed?
- Up or Left arrow key pressed?
- Close to a wall?
- On a square?

Input/output
- Move Taxi sprite

Process
- Lower speed
- Increase speed
- Calculate new position
- Apply consequence

Start/end
- End
- Start

(g) Include **two** of the following points:
- The default directions of flow are to the right or downwards.
- Each flow line should have an arrowhead at one end which shows the direction of flow.
- Flow lines join the symbols in a flow chart together.
- Flow lines show the paths that code can take through an algorithm.

2 (a)

First input	Second input	Expected output	Actual output
n	S	35	35
y	S	28	35
N	M	50	50
Y	M	40	50
N	p	75	0
Y	p	60	0

(b)
- Loop (UNTIL)
- Branch (IF THEN)

(c) Your answer should include **three** of the following points.
- Capitalisation becomes important for short inputs such as single characters or acronyms which are used in comparisons by code.
- If a text box is used for input there will be opportunities for the user to enter either upper or lower case.
- This can be handled using an ucase(), or lcase() to force the user input into the capitalisation needed by comparison code.
- The function could be used at the point of input if copied into a variable.
- The function could be used at the point of comparison
- An alternative approach can circumvent user typing by using a control such as a checkbox.
- An alternative approach can circumvent user typing by using a control such as a radio button.

(d) Your answer should include **four** of the following points. (The uses of rows and columns explained in this answer can be interchanged with no loss of marks.)
- The two dimensions of an array called 'Bookings' will provide an appropriate data structure for holding the attendances of members for the dancing sessions. One dimension, the rows, can be used for the members, and the other dimension, the columns, can be used for the sessions.
- The array can be used to hold text, which will make it a lot easier to use than numbers, as short abbreviations could be used to represent each member.
- An array allows a set of attendees for each session that can be accessed by a single identifier.
- The array will need to be saved to backing storage before the program is closed so data is not lost.
- The array will need to be opened from backing storage when the program is run to use previous entries.

(e)

	Array (1)	Array (2)	Array (3)	Array (4)	Array (5)	Array (6)
Before	NJ1	GM2	RE1	JM2	JB3	GM1
	GM2	NJ1	RE1	JM2	JB3	GM1
	GM2	NJ1	JM2	RE1	JB3	GM1
	GM2	NJ1	JM2	JB3	RE1	GM1
	GM2	NJ1	JM2	JB3	GM1	RE1
	GM2	JM2	NJ1	JB3	GM1	RE1
	GM2	JM2	JB3	NJ1	GM1	RE1
	GM2	JM2	JB3	GM1	NJ1	RE1
	GM2	JB3	JM2	GM1	NJ1	RE1
	GM2	JB3	GM1	JM2	NJ1	RE1
	GM2	GM1	JB3	JM2	NJ1	RE1
After	GM1	GM2	JB3	JM2	NJ1	RE1

(f) Your answer should include **two** of the following:
- MemberFee
- MemberType
- PreviousMember

Explanations could include:
- They may hold information needed in other parts of the program.
- They can be changed in other parts of the program.

(g) Your answer should include three of the following points
- A constant is very similar to a variable.
- The data held in a constant does not normally change as the program runs.
- A constant is appropriate for values such as a standard rate.
- The data held in a constant would usually be the same each time the code runs.

3 (a) Your answer should include two of the following errors with their fixes:
- ELSE statement will not reliably respond, to cut-out from a magazine, selected from the combo box.
  - Replace ELSE statement with IF Type = "cut-out"
- Statement to add a random number to the reference will overwrite the two-letter prefix. This line should add or concatenate the random number onto the prefix.
  - Replace Ref = Random() statement with Ref = Ref + Random()
- Allocating a random number should have a check that the number has not already been used or implement a different method such as incrementing the previous number.
  - Insert a WHILE loop around the Ref = Ref + Random() statement which iterates until a reference that has not already been used is found
- The pseudocode algorithm will not respond to printout being selected from the combo box.
  - Insert IF Type = "print out", Ref = "WP" lines of code

(b) Your answer should include:
- The first two letters of the reference can be used to sort items by type.
- The user can enter the first two letters to search for items of that type.

(c) Your answer should include the following:
- "CO" OR "HW" OR "PO" OR "PR" OR "WP"
- These are the only valid data entries so no other rules are needed.

(d) Arrays are appropriate data structures for the chef as these variables have many parts that are able to hold the data needed to keep track of recipes.

Single-dimensional arrays are a poor choice for this usage as at least three arrays would be needed to hold the

reference number, description and where the recipe is located. Synchronising these into the same order would be a little more difficult than multi-dimensional arrays, especially if sorting is coded into the program.

Multi-dimensional arrays is a good option with a choice of 2D or 3D arrays. A 2D array are conceptually rather like a spreadsheet table and easily able to store reference numbers, descriptions and where recipes are located. Using 2D could involve a separate array for each type of recipe or sorting one array on the reference. Using a 3D array could utilise the third dimension to hold each type of recipe.

(e) Program code needs to be able to output the recipes information to data file(s), otherwise any data in the arrays will be lost when the program closes. Similarly, this data needs to be input back into the program when it starts. Code to both output and input data will use loops to go through data. The output loop will use FOR as the number of recipes is known to the program. The input loop could use REPEAT or WHILE to keep the iteration until the end of file is reached, giving the flexibility needed to cater for different numbers of recipes.

The data file(s) will need to be opened before the loop and closed after. The open code statement will define whether the data is to be input or output.

A data file could be used for each type of recipe or they could be combined into one. If using one file, best to sort the data into types before saving to help code store them in the correct array(s).

4 (a) Line 4: Integer variable
Line 8: Multi-dimensional array of integers

(b)

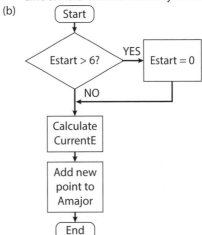

(c) Suggested answers could include
Object-orientated programming could be used to code Richard's problem using abstraction, inheritance and initial design for the program around real objects.

The program could be designed from an object-orientated approach, for example, the scales and fretboard being separate objects. Better use of objects can be from setting up the bass guitar neck as graphic objects for the strings and frets.

The first display could use abstraction to abstract the scale information from the scale object to display via the fret object. This will hide the details of how the fret displays are calculated.

Inheritance can be used to create the specific scale classes such as major or minor from a parent class of scales.

(d) Suggested answers could include
The code Richard has written can be improved in several ways.
- Objects should be given meaningful names. The code has a button named Button1, which does not help this or future programmers understand what the button is expected to do.

- The code should respond to combo boxes to define which scale and key are required. The code shown here is obviously prototyping the solution, so just focussing on making one scale work, but will need developing to respond to user inputs.
- The code starting "G string", "D string", "A string", "E string" has obvious duplications and should be improved by more careful coding.
- Code in each of these sections is repeated 8 times, so should be in a FOR loop to avoid the number of lines of code. This will also make it a lot easier to identify and fix any bugs.
- Bringing the repeated code into FOR loops can be further improved by using a subroutine to hold the loop. The subroutine can then be called from each string section using parameters to pass in the values for the start and current variables.
- Despite these issues there are some examples of good practice, in particular variables, which have meaningful names and are sensibly declared as local to this subroutine.

Answers to Revision test 2

1 (a) Your answer should include any **two** of the following:
- Random answer sequence to jumble up the choices of answers on the form.
- Checking for the correct answer to identify if the right choice has been made.
- Showing score to display the correct number of answer boxes and make a sound if the top score achieved.

(b)
```
BEGIN
IF Correct answer
        Set next score box to visible
        IF Break 100 score box is visible
                Sound winner music
                Start next level
ELSE
        IF score box to visible
                Set last score box to NOT visible
END
```

(c) Date/time: The date/time data type holds a point in time which could be used in the game to record when a level is started and finished, and therefore calculate how it took to complete.
Floating point (real): The floating point (also known as real) data type can be used to hold each calculated answer to the problems set for the user.
Integer: The integer data type can be used to keep track of how many problems have been answered correctly.

(d) Alphanumeric string: The alphanumeric string data type can hold many characters and is good for holding names, addresses and similar information.

String: The string data type is built upon alphanumeric to be able to hold control characters such as backspace as well as characters input from the keyboard.
Boolean: The Boolean data type is different to the other three in as much as it only holds one of two values, True or False, and is best used for conditions used for branching code.
Character: The other data types are all involved with characters that can be entered using a keyboard.
The character data type is exactly that, a place to keep a single character such as O or K or 3, useful to hold a single key press from the keyboard.

(e) A subscript is anything representing a number inside the brackets of an array. A subscript could be a number, variable or function. An 'Out of range' error can be generated when the subscript has a value which does not have a corresponding item in the array. Such an error can be caused if the subscript is larger than the number of items in the array.

(f) There are several patterns the program can use to help target future exercise questions. One easy pattern would be to set up questions into categories so those that have been answered incorrectly can be revisited.
The numbers used in the questions could be used so that areas that are identified as being difficult could use easier numbers for new questions, and made more difficult as the user grasps the concepts.
The amount of time needed to answer questions is another useful pattern, with quick responses showing little need for new questions in this category.

2 (a) Your answer should include **four** of the following terms:
- Variables are used to hold items of data while the program runs.
- Constants are similar to variables, except their data is not expected to change during program execution.
- Key processes are the subprograms needed within the system to make it work.
- Repeated processes are parts of the subprograms which need to iterate.
- Inputs are any key presses, mouse clicks, files or other inputs into the system.
- Outputs are any screen displays, printouts, sounds or other outputs from the system.

(b) A function is a named subprogram that returns a value. A function could be used:
- where code is needed to calculate a result
- where a subprogram is needed in code where a value is required.

A subroutine is a named subprogram that does not return a value. A subroutine could be used:
- where the same section of code is needed in different places within a program
- where a large subroutine needs breaking down into more manageable sections.

(c)

```
BEGIN CalculateDiscount (parameters: LastOrderDate, SalesInYear, OrderValue)
SET DiscountRate to ""
IF LastOrderDate within last 60 days OR SalesInYear >= SalesTarget OR OrderValue > ExtrasAmount
    SET DiscountRate to "C"
IF LastOrderDate within last 60 days AND SalesInYear >= SalesTarget
    SET DiscountRate to "B"
IF LastOrderDate within last 60 days AND OrderValue > ExtasAmount
    SET DiscountRate to "B"
IF OrderValue > ExtrasAmount AND SalesInYear >= SalesTarget
    SET DiscountRate to "B"
IF LastOrderDate within last 60 days AND SalesInYear >= SalesTarget AND OrderValue > ExtrasAmount
    SET DiscountRate to "A"
RETURN DiscountRate
END
```

(d) Your answer should include the following points:
- A global variable can be used anywhere in code to read what is in the variable.
- A global variable can be used anywhere in code to change what is in the variable.
- Any changes to the variable can be seen instantly by any other code.

(e) Your answer should include the following points:
- A While structure can keep iterating whilst the input is invalid.
- A While structure can complete when the input is good.
- Several lines of code can be inside the While loop, each validating an aspect of the data entry.

(f) Example answer

	000–199	200–399	400–599	600–799	800–999
AAD			✓	✓	✓
CSD		✓	✓		
GTH	✓			✓	
WWS			✓	✓	✓

(g)

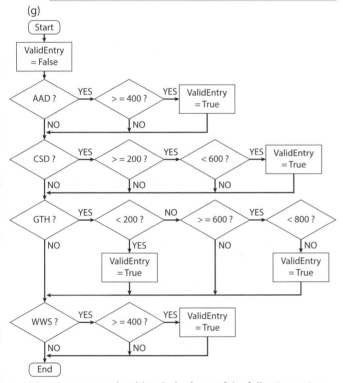

3 (a) Your answer should include **three** of the following points:
- Decomposition encourages the programming team to identify and describe the problems and processes involved in the system.
- Problems and processes can be broken down into distinct steps.
- Each distinct step can be described as a set of structured steps.
- Decomposition helps the programming team to communicate key features to other interested parties, such as the user management.

(b) Your answer should include the following points:
- Records are able to hold different data types for each customer.
- An array is limited to one data type.
- The different data types are name (alphanumeric), track dates/date of birth (date/time), lap times (floating point/ real).

(c)

	Array (1)	Array (2)	Array (3)	Array (4)	Array (5)	Array (6)
Before	35	12	36	27	20	4
	4	12	36	27	20	35
	4	12	27	36	20	35
	4	12	27	20	35	36
After	4	12	20	27	35	36

(d) • Your answer should include **eight** of the following points:
- Both bubble and quick sorts are standard algorithms used to sort data into a sequenced order.
- Bubble sort is best for small data sets.
- Bubble sort is much easier to understand.
- Bubble sort code iterates through the data, each time moving the largest item into its sorted place.
- Bubble sort is best where the programmer needs to be able to easily hack into parts of the code.
- Quick sort is the newer algorithm.
- Quick sort usually works a lot better.
- Quick sort is particularly suited to sorting large amounts of data.
- Quick sort algorithms use recursion, making this much harder to understand and to describe.
- Recursion is when a function calls itself.
- Recursion needs something to happen inside the function to end the recursion, otherwise it will never stop, with the computer freezing or crashing.
- The data in a quick sort is divided into two using a partition point, with recursion used to sort each side of this point.

4 (a) In this demonstration a binary search is made for item 4200 in a data set ordered from 1 to 8192.
The first comparison is 4200 with 4096 (half way between 1 and 8192) with 4200 in the upper half.
The next comparison is 4200 with 6144 (half way between 4096 and 8192) with 4200 in the lower half.
The next comparison is 4200 with 5120 (half way between 4096 and 6144) with 4200 in the lower half.
The next comparison is 4200 with 4608 (half way between 4096 and 5120) with 4200 in the lower half.
The next comparison is 4200 with 4352 (half way between 4096 and 4608) with 4200 in the lower half.
The next comparison is 4200 with 4224 (half way between 4096 and 4352) with 4200 in the lower half.
The next comparison is 4200 with 4160 (half way between 4096 and 4224) with 4200 in the upper half.
The next comparison is 4200 with 4192 (half way between 4160 and 4224) with 4200 in the upper half.
The next comparison is 4200 with 4208 (half way between 4192 and 4224) with 4200 in the lower half.
The next comparison is 4200 with 4200 (half way between 4192 and 4208) with 4200 found.

(b) </td> and </p> are in the wrong order, they need to be paired up with the <p> and <td> codes:
```
<td width="784" valign="top"
class="Body4"><p><strong>Party</strong>)
prices for catering
</p>
</td>
```

(c) Error 1: Line 6 has a typo with the name of the checkbox 'cherries', defined in line 22, shown as 'cherrys'. This can be corrected by changing line 6 from 'cherrys' to 'cherries'.
Error 2: Line 7 has an error in the calculation with the cost of this extra subtracted (price −= 2;) from the price. The extra should be added (price += 2;).
Error 3: Line 9 has an error in the calculation with the cost of cherries at £1 in this line of code, whereas line 23 shows the user the cost is £1.50. This can be corrected by changing line 9 from 'price += 1'; to 'price += 1.5';.

(d) Example answer:
The best code is written to meet the needs of the user, to work reliably and to be maintainable.
Meeting the needs of the user starts with good communication in order to clearly understand what is required from the app.
This should be followed by responding to user feedback when the software is used to resolve bugs and to enhance usability.
Designing and writing code to be maintainable is important and should be built into every app during every stage from early design through to actual deployment. The initial design should be very clear on how code is to be structured, with the use of variables defined and functionalities and interactions between the subprograms understood and documented.
When the code is written a great deal of care should be taken in naming objects, variables and subprograms. The goal here is to produce code which reads as close to English as possible, so current and future programmers can easily understand what the code does.
Comments should be used to annotate code, to summarise what sections of the code do and to clarify areas which are less clear, such as the basis for decision making.
Technical documentation should clearly define the workings of the code.
Technical documentation should track revisions.
Technical documentation should record all testing with amendments needed to rectify any failed tests.
Technical documentation should record any bug-fixing.

Other correct answers are possible.

Unit 2: Fundamentals of Computer Systems

Answers to Revision test 1

1 (a)

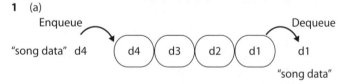

Song data is added to the back of the buffer and played from the front in order.

(b) A queue is the most natural data structure because a queue enables tracks to be added at the back and taken off and played from the front. It can grow and shrink as tracks are added and played – they are deleted (dequeued) from the queue as soon as they have been played.

(c) A list

(d) A playlist

(e)

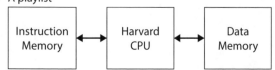

(f) A Real Time Operating System as this is essentially an embedded system which requires fast processing of inputs in a predictable manner.

(g)

A	B	C	A.B	B.C	A.B+B.C
0	0	0	0	0	0
0	0	1	0	0	0
0	1	0	0	0	0
0	1	1	0	1	1
1	0	0	0	0	0
1	0	1	0	0	0
1	1	0	1	0	1
1	1	1	1	1	1

(h)

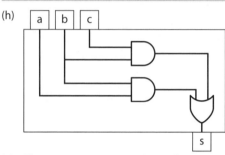

2 (a) The magnetic stripe on the card contains identification data. The card reader reads this data and then compares the data against a database of ID numbers. If the ID is authorised it allows entry.

(b) It is the card that is identified, not the user, so it would be possible for unauthorised people to gain access. It is more of a problem for staff who keep their cards for a long time than visitors who have to hand the card in at the end of their visit.

(c) Biometric fingerprint scan for staff. This would mean staff would not have to carry their cards and therefore, potentially lose them and they would be unambiguously identified. This involves using a camera to scan the fingerprint and record its pattern in the database. After this, staff will touch their fingerprint on a reader at each entry point. This will scan the fingerprint and compare it to the biometric database.
Visitors could be given a chip and pin card. This could be programmed in the system in such a way that the visitor would only be allowed to enter and leave during a fixed time period.

(d) Backing up involves making a copy of the live data in case the data is destroyed, lost or corrupted as a result of a deliberate malicious act, such as a virus, or the actions of a disgruntled employee or other system user, or as a result of an unanticipated system event, disc failure or an accident. In the event of a mishap or malicious act the live data would be lost and this may cause, at best, great inconvenience to the firm and, at worst, factory closure.
Archiving is a different process. It is not concerned with live data but with keeping data for the long term. It involves keeping a separate, often offline, copy of the data safely just in case it is ever required for inspection or use in the future. This will often be undertaken when the firm no longer needs the live data and/or when more space is needed on the main disc drives.
Backup should be performed regularly on the live data so that no live data is lost.
It is important to have a standard set of procedures that is documented and followed without fail.

A possible set of procedures would be:
- Maintain a RAID 5 system for fault tolerance.
- Backup the whole system incrementally every day to a backup hard drive.
- Keep each day's backup for the week, then rewrite these the following week.
- Every week, perform a full system backup onto the backup hard drive and take a copy onto removable storage, such as a DVD/RW which is taken off premises and stored in a fireproof safe.
- Maintain weekly copies of the backup through the month. At the end of each month keep a monthly copy and rewrite the weekly copies in order.
- Archive the data to DVD/RW every year when the live data is no longer required.

(e)
$$\begin{bmatrix} 10 & 20 & 10 \\ 5 & 6 & 5 \end{bmatrix} + \begin{bmatrix} 4 & 3 & 4 \\ 3 & 4 & 4 \end{bmatrix} = \begin{bmatrix} 10+4 & 20+3 & 10+4 \\ 5+3 & 6+4 & 5+4 \end{bmatrix}$$
$$= \begin{bmatrix} 14 & 23 & 14 \\ 8 & 10 & 9 \end{bmatrix}$$

(f)
$$\begin{bmatrix} 2 \\ 3 \end{bmatrix}^T = \begin{bmatrix} 2 & 3 \end{bmatrix}$$

(g)
$$\begin{bmatrix} 2 & 3 \end{bmatrix} \begin{bmatrix} 14 & 23 & 14 \\ 8 & 10 & 9 \end{bmatrix} = \begin{bmatrix} 14*2 & 23*2 & 14*2 \\ + & + & + \\ 8*3 & 10*3 & 9*3 \end{bmatrix}$$
$$= \begin{bmatrix} 52 & 76 & 55 \end{bmatrix}$$

The revenue would be £52 for January, £76 for February and £55 for March.

3 (a) RAM because most instructions and data are accessed by the CPU from the RAM.

(b) The system bus is a combination of the data bus (which carries data to and from memory and I/O), the address bus (which holds the address the data is stored at and is used to fetch data and instructions), and the control bus (which carries control signals to and from the control unit).

(c) Speeding up the clock will make the processor work faster. However, in general terms the clock is set at a speed which is suitable for the system. Overclocking may cause overheating, and thus reliability problems, or even system failure.

(d) FETCH:
- Contents of PC copied to MAR
- Address bus used to go to address in MAR
- Contents of that memory location loaded into the MDR via data bus
- Increment contents of PC to point at next instruction
- Transfer content of MDR to the CIR

DECODE:
- Decode instruction held by the CIR
- The control unit decodes the instruction; instruction split into opcode and operand

EXECUTE:
- The opcode identifies the type of instruction it is and control unit controls execution
- Instruction executed
- Result stored in accumulator
- If instruction is a jump then PC is updated with the jump address.

(e) It is possible to emulate other systems using an emulator. Software is available on Unix systems that can emulate other proprietary systems, such as Windows systems or Apple Macintosh systems, whose kernel is itself based on a distribution of Unix.

If the CPU that is used for the proprietary system is the same or slower and less complex than the system running the software, the emulation can potentially be quite successful.

In this case, the system and CPU would be capable of running other proprietary systems so it would be possible to emulate these systems. On the other hand, it is a dual core processor which is not the latest technology and could therefore not be expected to cope very well with some of the very latest games.

The operating system for the target system could be loaded onto the source system and then the target system could be run on the system. Software for the target system could then be loaded and run to work with the emulated OS.

However, the translation involved in doing this does mean that the target software will run more slowly than it would in its native manner. If the software is not particularly time or feedback sensitive, this probably would not matter greatly. If the screen took a second to update a calculation in a spreadsheet rather a few milliseconds, it would be irritating but possibly manageable.

If the software requires feedback to operate, such as in drawing a line, or filling a shape or shooting at a target, the delay could be very irritating as the user is not sure whether the processor has carried out the operation and the user adjusts too quickly, causing errors that have to be corrected.

As Reskey wants it to emulate games this is potentially a major problem. Most games require fast reactions to visual feedback and very fast graphics processing. These are areas that emulation is not good for and why it is usually only possible to emulate successfully when a much faster processor is emulating a much slower one.

The other major area which could be a big disappointment is the I/O hardware. Reskey has specified a touch screen display and a mouse. This is fine for games targeted at a touch screen and/or mouse but would not be useful for the latest games for the two systems which would need dedicated controllers.

Emulating add-on hardware is a particular challenge as the source and target (through the source) operating systems may have some conflict in dealing with interrupts from the controllers. Even when the controllers are well managed, there will be delay in handling these which will cause some issues unless the source CPU is much faster than the target. Games software is notorious for bypassing the standard operating system and writing code directly to the CPU in order to, for example, speed up processing of I/O. Although this is less necessary and indeed less possible on very modern systems, where it has been done, the emulation will almost certainly fail.

In summary, the idea of using this system under Unix to emulate other advanced proprietary systems, particularly running CPU and GPU intensive software which requires specialist I/O hardware, is really not a viable option. At best, it would allow a flavour of the games and, at worst, they would not play.

4 (a) A simplex channel

(b) A handshake sets up how two devices will communicate with each other. It specifies the details that both devices will use such as type of transfer, speed of transfer in bps, error checking.

(c)
0101 0110	V
0110 0101	e
0110	6
1001	9
1001	9
0001	1

The code transmitted is Ve6991

(d) Source address: The address (IP address) of the server in California from which the maps data is sent.
Destination address: The address of the PC that is downloading the data where the downloaded packets have to be routed to.
Payload: The downloaded data itself divided and put into packets. The packets can be routed in different directions around the internet to the destination, taking different times and be reassembled at the destination.
Sequence number: Describes which element of the sequence a particular packet is when it is split up, so that it can be reassembled at the destination even if the packets arrive in the wrong order – one may take longer to arrive as a result of a dropped packet or a longer route.
Checksum: An error detection item. The TCP/IP software at each router recomputes the checksum from the packet and compares it against the received checksum. If it is ok it sends an ACK, otherwise it waits for a resend.

Answers to Revision test 2

1 (a) Reason 1. There are a restricted number of options a user can take so it is easier to use a system where the number of options is restricted rather than having a flexible system.
Reason 2. It will be faster and easier to learn on a menu-based interface.
(b) The bar code is a series of black and white lines starting and ending with guard lines so that the scanner knows where to start and stop.
The data lines encode the digits of the bar code and a check digit.
The scanner detects the reflected light from these lines and generates an analog voltage.
An analogue to digital converter changes this to a series of digital digits.
(c) A check digit is added to the series of digits when the bar code is generated. An algorithm is applied to the series of digits that are read in and if it yields the correct result the number is presented, otherwise an error is signalled.
(d) A numeric keypad (or touch display virtual numeric keypad).
(e) 1. A NAS is simple to set up and operate as an in-house cloud storage device, suitable for storing the large quantities of data that would derive from an HD colour video system.
2. It offers relatively inexpensive, fault-tolerant storage backup of data.
(f) Advantage: RAID 1 offers fault tolerance through copying the same data onto two identical (mirror) discs. If one fails then the other disc still holds all the data.
Disadvantage: It takes 2 GB of actual storage to store 1 GB of data as all data is mirrored. As a video system will generate large volumes of data this could become uneconomic.
(g) Your answer should include:
Running a five-disc RAID 5 configuration:
• RAID systems allow inexpensive hardware to be used for large-volume fault-tolerant systems.
• RAID 5 uses striping across five discs, with four discs holding data and then the fifth holding parity data for the four items of data in the stripe.
• The video data and parity data are distributed across the five discs. If any disc fails then it can be rebuilt automatically by using the data on the remaining four discs.
• Using five discs means that there is approximately a 20 per cent overhead for storing the parity data, so it is a lot more economical than using RAID 1 with its mirror system.
• On the other hand, if two discs fail at the same time (or while the first is being rebuilt) then it is not possible to reconstruct the data.
• If the wrong disc is swapped out, the data will be corrupted.

• In this case, as it is being used to backup important shared data it will provide a good degree of fault tolerance in a fast and secure way in a relatively inexpensive manner.
2 (a) Reason 1. Symmetric key encryption uses the same key for encrypting as well as for decrypting data. It is therefore very simple to use.
Reason 2. If sufficient bits are used for encryption it is extremely secure. In effect, it is totally uncrackable given today's level of technology. The ciphertext cannot be decrypted without knowing the private key.
(b) When establishing a secure connection between the client and the store's server, the transaction itself is conducted over public telecommunications lines that potential hackers can see. The key must be passed between the server and client, which means that there is potential for it to be seen.
(c) The customer's browser will use this public key to establish a secure connection with the server that is hosting the secure page in the following way.
• The browser has a list of preinstalled trusted servers.
• The server gives the browser its digital certificate from one of these trusted servers.
• The browser generates a private key based on the public key in the server's certificate.
• The browser uses a symmetric key to encrypt the data, and uses the private key that was previously generated in order to encrypt the symmetric key.
• The browser then transmits the symmetric key and the encrypted data to the server.
• The server decrypts the symmetric key using its own matched public key.
• It then uses this to decrypt the data.
(d) JPEG
(e) PNG
(f) PGP should retain the original files because:
• JPEG is a lossy format.
• image information will be lost and it may be needed, for example, when a poster is wanted.
• Metadata may be lost which could be useful later. Metadata includes details of the exposure, f-stops, data, place etc.
• The original images cannot be displayed on most Web browsers; even where this is possible the data transmission time would be excessive.
• The main JPEG file can be optimised for quality against storage space and will therefore load relatively quickly on a web browser even on a slow connection.
• The thumbnail file will take very little storage space but can be optimised for its size.
(g) The original illustration file should be kept for:
• future editing in the original format
• keeping it in a bitmap format rather than a vector format could lead to scaling issues when the file is used in a different context,.
3 (a)

(Note the unidirectional nature of the address bus.)
(b) The clock generates a system event in the control unit. Each tick of the clock generates the next step in each phase of the fetch decode execute cycle.

(c) The clock can be speeded up, thus making the CPU work more quickly. This is the process of 'overclocking. However, this can lead to overheating problems and may make the system less reliable.

(d) The Von Neumann bottleneck is a limitation of conventional stored program architecture computers as a result of both instructions and data being fetched across the same data bus. The much faster processor is slowed down by the speed of transfer as it is always waiting for data to be fetched.

Both cluster computing and multi-core processing are forms of parallel processing and are both suitable, if somewhat different, strategies for overcoming the Von Neumann bottleneck.

Cluster computing is a form of distributed processing. It comprises a group of potentially less powerful computers connected together, tightly or less tightly, over a network, all operating together under software control to perform a task or tasks.

Conceptually, using this form of parallel cluster computing manages to overcome the bottleneck. It is able to deal well with a complex task broken down into a set of smaller tasks or deal with a number of different tasks in a multi-tasking environment. The main advantages are that each local system has access to its own and shared resources, such as memory, which can be coordinated via the controlling software. There is less conflict on resources than in a single processor environment and it is very scalable. If processing power slows down, another CPU-based system can be added.

On the negative side, distributed resources require more coordination, processing power and specialised software to coordinate. Using remote resources, such as memory, is slower than using local resources and therefore some of the advantages of avoiding the bottleneck can be lost.

Multi-core processing is a different form of parallel processing in which there are multiple processing units on a single chip all sharing the same memory (UMA). These could potentially exacerbate the von Neumann bottleneck as they require even more processing power for the same memory.

However, the chips are designed with this in mind. They have many different levels of cache memory in order to avoid having to throughput substantial amounts of data so often on the bus. They are therefore able to avoid having the same degree of bottleneck. They also are set up to run tasks and threads in parallel, again making best use of processor time relative to the data being sent through. On the cautionary side, this only works if the operating systems and software have been written to take advantage of the caching and parallelism that are possible, which is not always the case.

Both cluster computing and multi-core processing are potentially effective strategies for dealing with the Von Neumann bottleneck if the software that runs on them is set up optimally for parallel processing.

4 (a) Sorting in time of departure order.

(b) 1100 1100 1 Even parity – 10 Upper case 01100 12th letter L
0100 0111 0 Even parity – 10 Upper case 00111 7th letter G
1101 0111 1 Even parity – 10 Upper case 10111 23rd letter W
The Message is LGW

(c) 1100 0111 has five 1s and fails the even parity check and a resend request would be sent.

(d) A queue

(e) It is a FIFO structure. The aircraft would be dealt with in the order they are scheduled. It would not be so suitable if the order were changed regularly whilst the aircraft were waiting to land.

(f) An RTOS would be most useful. Your reasoning should include some or all of the following:
- The OS has to deal with inputs in a reliable and totally predictable manner without any unnecessary delay, which would be potentially disastrous for an aircraft.
- The inputs and output peripherals are known, and the results of input parameters need to be totally predictable.
- There is a reliance on sensor data and feedback.
- They are small and ultra-reliable systems.
- Reliance on hardware for speed of response and predictability.

Unit 3: Planning and Management of Computing Projects

Revision task 1

Answers to Revision activity 1

Project details

Project title	Training Recording System
Project sponsor name	Mike Glaslyn, Managing Director
Client name	Kirsty Glaslyn, Finance Director
Project manager name	[Your name]
Start date	1 August 2017
Completion date	31 August 2017
Estimated cost	£80 000

Document details

Version	Modifications	Author	Date
2	Project budget update, Software Developer additional cost	Kirsty Glaslyn	July

Document approvals

Name	Role	Signature	Date	Version
Kirsty Glaslyn	Finance Director	*Kirsty Glaslyn*	July	2
Mike Glaslyn	Managing Director	*Mike Glaslyn*	July	2

Document distribution

Name	Role	Date of Issue	Version
Mike Glaslyn	Managing Director	July	2
Kirsty Glaslyn	Finance Director	July	2
Wayne Applewood	Training Manager	July	2
Samira Khan	Software Team Manager	July	2

Purpose of the Project Initiation Document

Project aims:
Suggested answers could include:
- To provide an integrated linked system that will allow the training provider to record details of the course, Trainer/Assessor and client.
- To enable customers to search, book and pay for courses online.
- To generate invoices when the customer books a course.
- To provide an electronic training events schedule or diary.
- To enable customer to update their own details online.

You could also add the benefits of implementing the new system such as:

- Save money, improve customer service and productivity and to grow the business and improve accuracy.
- Provide access to new markets and increase sales.

Project management and control:
Suggested answers could include:

- Acceptance testing as part of the quality and review process.
- Tester/Assessor to use user acceptance testing as part of the quality and review process.
- Software Tester to use ISO/IEC 25010:2011 standard to test the new system.
- Training Manager and Software Team Manager to support the System Installations technicians in the quality checking process to ensure that the new system works as expected.

Background to the Proposed Work:

Your answer should include:

- The company does not have the facility for organisations and individuals to search for courses, book and pay for courses online.
- Manual system is time consuming and not accurate.
- To integrate and automate all of the systems.

Objectives

Suggested answers could include:

SMART Objective	Achieved?	Date and comments
Project start date 1 August	Yes	Project started successfully on the 1 August
Project launch 1 September	Yes	Project launched on the 1 September
System installed by system installations 29 August	Yes	System installed successfully
Project to be completed within the allocated £80 000 budget	Yes	The project was completed under budget £77 434
A return of £1500 at the end of 1 year	No	Return of £1000 at the end of 1 year
increase on course sales revenue of at least 20% at the end of 1 year	No	An increase on course sales revenue of 15% at the end of 1 year
Customers able to search, book and pay for courses online 31 August	Yes	Customers are able to search, book and pay for courses online
Automated invoice sent to customer when course booked online from 1 September	No	Technical issue has occurred. The system allowed the customer to book the course online, but it did not send the invoice to the customer's email address for the payment of the course or link to the company accounts system.
Customer satisfaction improved to 90%	Yes	Customer satisfaction improved to 90% and records are accurate
Administrative costs reduced by 10% within the next 3 months	Yes	Administrative costs have also reduced by 15% within 2 months.
Course occupancy is greater than the targeted 95% within the next 6 months	Yes	Course occupancy is greater than the targeted 96% within the next 5 months

Scope

Suggested answers could include:

- Organisations and individuals to book and pay for courses online
- Integrate and automate all of the systems
- Electronic schedule diary
- Customer facility to update details online
- Will not cover online course

Assumptions

Suggested answers could include:

Assumption	Validated by	Status	Comments
The staff will be able to use the new system	Training Manager	Marginal	Additional training will be given
Hardware and software compatibility	Software Team Manager	Confirmed	Hardware and software updated
System Installations will install the new system	Software Team Manager	Confirmed	Server contractor confirmed installation schedule and costs
Software bugs removed after testing	Software Team Manager	Confirmed	ISO/IEC 25010:2011, and end user testing. Software Team Manager, Training Manager and system installation contractor will ensure quality installation
Supplier delivers hardware on time	Project Manager Server contractor	Confirmed	Delivery schedule agreed
Training Manager and Software Team Manager will be able to support the System Installations Technicians	Project Manager	Open	Assuming that the Training Manager and Software Team Manager are available and provide the required support
The installation will be completed within the allotted 3 days	Server contractor	Open	Assuming no unforeseen problems arise

Constraints

Suggested answers could include:

Constraint	Validated by	Status	Comments
The service contractor will be able to supply the hardware and software within budget and quality	Software Team Manager	Critical	Alternative suppliers sourced to ensure that alternative hardware and software can be purchased within budget and of the required quality
ISO/IEC 25010:2011 standard to test the new system	Software Team Manager	Critical	System must follow ISO/IEC 25010:2011 standard to ensure that the system is fully operational and compliant

Risk management strategy

Suggested answers could include:

Risk	Probability	Impact	Severity	Contingency Plan
The service contractor goes bankrupt	Medium	High	Critical	New supplier and installation company secured
Hardware and software compatibility	Low	Medium	Marginal	Purchase compatible hardware
The installation will take 3 days	Medium	High	Marginal	More staff made available for the installation
Software bugs not removed in testing process	Low	Medium	Critical	Further testing carried out

Deliverables

Suggested answers could include:

Item	Components	Description
Online Training Booking System	Training event diary	Link to Trainer/Assessor and course diaries and invoice system
Training events diary	Trainer diary	A diary that record all of the training events, training details and venue details.

Project quality strategy

Suggested answers could include:

Stakeholders	Responsibility
Managing Director	Project sponsor – provides the authority and guidance, and maintains the priority of the project in the organisation Control of finance
Project Manager	Responsible for defining, planning, controlling and leadership
Finance Director	Client – provides the product requirements and project finance
Software Team Manager	Responsible for following company policies
Server contractor	Supplies materials and equipment Contributes specialist work

Communication Plan

Suggested answers could include:

Stakeholder(s)	Frequency	Type	Purpose
Managing Director	Weekly	Email informing them of the project status.	Keep the Managing Director (project sponsor) informed of progress to date
Finance Director	Weekly	Risk assessments, Project Checkpoint and work tolerance status Email reports	Keep the Finance Director (client) informed of progress to date
Software Team Manager	Daily	Delivery schedule updates Testing process update Email updates	Keep the Software Team Manager updated on the testing process

Answers to Revision activity 2

(a)

Gantt chart — Days (1–31)

Project stages	1	2	3	4	5	6	7	8	9	10	11	12	13	14	15	16	17	18	19	20	21	22	23	24	25	26	27	28	29	30	31
Start up	█																														
Analysis		░	░	◇																											
Design				█	█	█	◇																								
Development								░	░	░	░	░	░	░	░	░	░	░	░	░	░	░	◇ ░	░	░	░	░	◇			
																													░	░	
Handover																															◇ █

(b)

Resource list:
Server hardware
Microsoft Windows server
Microsoft SQL server
Web development software
Microsoft Office
Laptops (4)
System Installations costs
Software Team Manager equipment rental
Software Developer equipment rental
Webpage Developer equipment rental

Staffing list:
Server contractor Software Developer
Project Manager
Business Analyst
Software Team Manager
Webpage Developer
Software Tester
Training Manager
Trainer/Assessor

(c) Cost plan

Training recording system budget	£80 000		
Hardware and software	**Amount**	**Item cost (£)**	**Total cost (£)**
Server hardware	1	2300	2300
Microsoft Windows server	1	2750	2750
Microsoft SQL server	1	2356	2356
Web development software	1	510	510
Microsoft Office	1	167	167
Laptop computers	4	699	2796
Total Hardware and software cost			**10 879**

Project team	**Daily hrs**	**Hr cost (£)**	**5-days testing (£)**	**26 days (£)**	**31 days (£)**
Project Manager	6.5	50	1625	8450	10 075
Business Analyst	6.5	48	1560	8112	9672
Software Team Manager	6.5	42	1365	7098	8463
Software Developer	6.5	32	1040	5408	6448
Webpage Developer	6.5	32	1040	5408	6448
Software Tester	6.5	25	812.50	4225	5037.50
Training Manager	6.5	39	1267.50	6591	7858.50
Trainer/Assessor	6.5	24	780	4056	4836
Total Project team costs			**Total cost 9490**	**49 348**	**58 838**

System installation	**Amount**	**Item cost (£)**	**One-off cost (£)**
System installation costs	1	850	850
Server contractor Software Developer	1	600	600
Components from another supplier	1	855	855
Total System installations costs			**2305**

Functional points	**Daily hrs**
Course Schedule module interface	5
Payment module	2
Trainer/Assessor module	3
Venue module	3
Client services	3
Reporting module	3
Total Functional points	**19**

Additional costs per functional point	**Daily hrs**	**FP**	**Hours**	**Costs (£)**
Software Team Manager	2	19	38	1596
Software Developer	1	19	19	608
Webpage Developer	0.5	19	9.5	304
Software Tester	0.5	19	9.5	238
Total Additional costs per functional point				**2746**

Equipment rental pro-rata cost	**6.5-hour day (£)**	**Days**	**Costs (£)**
Software Team Manager	24	31	744
Software Developer	19	31	589
Webpage Developer	24	31	744
Software Tester	19	31	589
Total Equipment rental pro-rata cost			**2666**

Total project cost	**£77 434**
Budget	**£80 000**
Project under budget by	**£2566**

Answers to Revision activity 3

Project Checkpoint Report (PCR)
Suggested answers could include:

Report Details

Date of Checkpoint:	27 August 2017
Period Covered:	End of User Testing

Version	Modifications	Author	Date
2	Webpage Developer's Course Schedule database update requires an additional 2 days Gantt chart updated	Project Manager	23 August
3	Increase in the cost of components £855 Project budget updated	Finance Manager	25 August

Document approvals

Name	Role	Signature	Date	Version
Mike Glaslyn	Managing Director	*Mike Glaslyn*	30 August	3
Kirsty Glaslyn	Finance Director	*Kirsty Glaslyn*	30 August	3

Document distribution

Name	Role	Date of Issue	Version
Mike Glaslyn	Managing Director	30 August	3
Kirsty Glaslyn	Finance Director	30 August	3
[Your name]	Project Manager	30 August	3
Wayne Applewood	Training Manager	30 August	3

Products

Product Name	Work Undertaken	Date Complete
Online training booking system	Testing of the online training booking system to ensure that it is free of errors	22 August
Training event diary	Testing of the Training event diary to see that it can be updated and accessed. All course bookings reflected on online training booking system	22 August
Invoice system	Testing of the Invoice system to ensure that an invoice is generated and emailed to the customer when a customer books a course. Also updated entry on the sales ledger.	22 August

Quality Management
Suggested answers could include:
- The server contractor builds the computer and server as per specification.
- The Software Team Manager supported the Software Tester to use ISO/IEC 25010:2011 standard to test the new system.
- The Tester/Assessor helped with acceptance testing.

Work package tolerance status
You could include:

Time:	5 days
Cost:	Staff costs approx. £9490
Quality:	Testing: The Software Team Manager supported the software tester to use ISO/IEC 25010:2011 standard to test the new system. Assessor helped with acceptance testing.

Issues Log

Date Raised	Raised By	Description	Action Taken	Date Closed
23 August	Software Team Manager	The Webpage Developer is still updating the Course Schedule database the expected delay is 2 days.	The Trainer/Assessor was asked to help the Webpage Developer update the Course Schedule database.	August
25 August	Finance Director	Server contract has had problems obtaining components for the computer.	Purchased the components from another supplier at an additional cost of £855	August

Answers to Revision activity 4

Your evaluation could cover the following points.

Email	
From	[Your name]
To	Mike Glaslyn, Managing Director
Subject	Project close (Training Recording System)

Dear Mike

Start up

The project started on time on 1 August 2017 and all of the resources and staff allocated to each task. The Gantt chart supported the planning process and was issued to each stakeholder. The Project Initiation Document identified the purpose and requirements of the project with SMART targets, risk management strategy and a clear communication plan.

Analysis stage

The Business Analyst worked with the Training Manager to carry out the analysis of the current manual systems and created the requirements specifications. This stage was completed within the estimated three days, no issues reported.

Design stage

The Business Analyst and Software Team Manager worked together to design the new system.

Server contractor's Software Developer helped in the design stage of the project. This stage of the project was carried out successfully and on time.

Development stage

The Software Team Manager monitored the Software Developer, Webpage Developer and Software Tester in the development of the new system.

Two issues identified during this stage

1. On 23 August 2017 the Webpage Developer reported a two day delay in updating the Course Schedule database. The update was taking longer than expected.
2. On 25 August 2017 the server contractor reported problems in obtaining components for the computer and has purchased the components from another supplier.

The Webpage Developer could not update the Course Schedule database within the allocated time. One of the Trainer/Assessors had to support him in this process. I would recommend that more time is given to updating information in the next project or more staff allocated to the task, to ensure it is completed successfully and on time.

The additional cost of £855 for the server components added to the costs of the project.

This stage of the project went over budget and over time.

User testing

Software Tester used ISO/IEC 25010:2011 standard to successfully test the new system. However, a few bugs remained on system launch. Further consideration should be given to the testing strategy in the next project, such as clarifying the testing requirements and the standard to be used.

Asking the Trainer/Assessor to be a part of the user acceptance testing as part of the quality and review process worked well, as the Assessor understood the business and user need of the system.

Installation

The server contractor installed the hardware and software for the project. Additional costs occurred for the component. Further research into sourcing components should be carried out for the next project to ensure that the component is compatible and available by the required date.

Direct changeover did not go well; the Course Training Schedule would not update. Next time a more detailed list of requirements should be sourced to ensure that we understand the updates requirement of all systems.

The system now allowed the customer to book the course online, but it did not send the invoice to the customer's email address for the payment of the course or link to the company accounts system. This will be investigated further.

Handover

Project costs approximately £77 434, just under budget. The additional cost of sourcing the server components and updating the Course Schedule database did not affect the budget.

Staff were able to use new integrated new training recording system when they returned to work on 1 September 2017.

The hardware was capable of processing all of the data requirements of the new training recording system.

We should also consider other system implementation stages. We used direct changeover this time but if the system was bigger, a staged implementation might be advised to ensure that each section was implemented and working before the next stage was implemented.

Recommend a more detailed contingency plan next time, even though it was not required. We should accommodate the requirement of all systems, hardware and software resources.

Further support is also required to cover for the lack of in-house technical expertise, to address the legal issues of securing the trainer and storing customer details. Ongoing support costs should be investigated.

We had good feedback. The Training Manager reported that the online system has allowed him to manage the course bookings and that the monitoring of the course occupancy was easier, and that it was greater than the targeted 96 per cent within five months.

The Training Manager could also plan for further courses as he can see the Trainer/Assessor's availability on the electronic diary.

Customer satisfaction has improved to 90 per cent – customers' records are accurate as they are updated by the customers themselves.

Expected business benefit of the project has materialised and measurable improvement in course sales and customer satisfaction have been seen:

- Course occupancy of at least 95 per cent within six months.
- Customer satisfaction improved to 90 per cent.
- Administrative costs reduced by 15 per cent within two months.
- Automate processes Improve accuracy.
- Course occupancy is 96 per cent, greater than the targeted 95 per cent and within four months.
- Improved Training Manager reporting on course occupancy.
- See Assessor's availability on the electronic diary.

Lessons learned

- Ensure sufficient time and staff are allocated to updating the existing system. Next time a more detailed list of requirements should be sourced to ensure that we understand the updates requirement of all systems.
- Further testing is required to ensure that the invoice is emailed to customers and linked to the company accounts system.
- Ensure that suppliers are able to deliver the goods ordered at agreed cost.
- Consider other changeover methods due to the high risk of direct changeover.
- Recommend a more detailed contingency plan next time, even though it was not required. We should accommodate the requirement of all systems, hardware and software resources.

Conclusion

The project was completed successfully and within budget. Some elements of the system are not fully operational but are ongoing. The majority of the project aims were fulfilled by the project.

Regards
[Your name]

[Your name]

Revision task 2

Answers to Revision activity 1

Project Initiation Document

Project details

Project title	Fresh Sport Dynasty online ordering system
Project Sponsor name	Paula Worthy, Managing Director
Client name	Max Clarke, Marketing Manager
Project Manager name	[Your name]
Start date	9 October 2017
Completion date	26 December 2017
Estimated cost	£200 000

Document details

Version	Modifications	Author	Date
2	Budget update cost of hardware and software and installation	Allan MacInnes	18 October
2	Gantt chart updated due to new installation date	[Your name]	20 October

Document approvals

Name	Role	Signature	Date	Version
Paula Worthy	Managing Director	*Paula Worthy*	20 October	2
Sonal Paun	Networking Service Director	*Sonal Paun*	20 October	2
Allan MacInnes	Finance Director	*Allan MacInnes*	20 October	2

Document distribution

Name	Role	Date of Issue	Version
Paula Worthy	Managing Director	20 October	2
Sonal Paun	Networking Service Director	20 October	2
Allan MacInnes	Finance Director	20 October	2
Tom Kotulski	Software Team Manager	20 October	2
Anna Hayton	Quality Manager	20 October	2
George Afua	Business Manager	20 October	2

Purpose of the Project Initiation Document

Project aims:
Suggested answers could include:

- Provide the business with a new stock control system and online shopping facility.
- Online ordering system to access new markets.
- Use customer intelligence to understand customer needs.
- Enable a comprehensive view of consumer purchases by products sales analysis.
- Satisfy the customer needs better than the competition.

Project management and control

- ISO/IEC 25010:2011 standard to work on the project.
- World Wide Web Consortium (W3C®).

Background to the proposed work

The company does not have an online shopping facility and the Managing Director is keen to move into this area of the of retail market.

The current stock control system has become difficult to update and it does not provide any information on consumer purchases. Therefore it has become difficult to analyse customer sales.

Objectives
Suggested answers include:

SMART Objective	Achieved?	Date and comments
Project allocated 11 weeks, start date 9 October	Yes	Project start date 9 October
Increase sales by 15% within 1 year	Yes	An increase of 30% in the online sales of sports fitness equipment was also seen
Reduce overheads by 10% within 6 months	Yes	The new system reduced overheads by 10% within 4 months
A return of at least £7500 at the end of 3 years	Yes	The expected return of at least £7500 at the end of 3 years did not occur. The actual return was £6000
Increase the number of orders handled from 15 per day to at least 30 per day within 3 months	No	It took longer, 4 months to increase the number of orders handled from 15 per day to at least 30 per day
Complete project by 17 December 2017	No	The project was launched on 15 January, 4 week late

Scope
The new online ordering system will provide the business with a new stock control system. This will allow the company to carry out a comprehensive view of consumer purchases by products sales analysis, which will enable it to satisfy customer needs better than the competition.

The new system must be launched on 26 December to take advantage of Christmas store closures and the start of the January sales.

The online facility will not include a section on the website for customers to provide product reviews. This will be scheduled for the next stage of the project.

Assumptions
Suggested answers include:

Assumption	Validated by	Status	Comments
Business Analyst creates accurate requirements specifications	Managing Director	Open	Cannot be confirmed until the end of the project
Hardware and software will be able to process the online sales website	Networking Service Director	Confirmed	The server contractor has guaranteed that the hardware and software will be able to process the online sales website
Testing will result in a fully functional system	Networking Service Director	Confirmed	The testers are aware of the business and user requirements
Will increase exposure to the online retail market to provide access to new markets	Managing Director	Open	The exposure to the online retail market should be investigated further
Project completed within budget	Finance Director	Open	Final costs to be calculated at the end of the project
All project stages will be completed on time	Project Manager	Open	To be monitored
The system will provide a comprehensive view of consumer purchases	Finance Director	Open	To be monitored
Implementation via pilot changeover for the sales of sports fitness equipment will be successful	Networking Service Director	Confirmed	Pilot changeover successful
Will be able to secure customer details	Networking Service Director	Confirmed	Legal issues of securing customer details addressed

Constraints

Constraint	Validated by	Status	Comments
World Wide Web Consortium (W3C®)	Anna Hayton, Quality Manager	Marginal	Other testing strategies could be used for the webpage testing
ISO/IEC 25010:2011	Anna Hayton, Quality Manager	Marginal	Other testing strategies could be used for the software testing

Risk management strategy

Suggested answers include:

Risk	Probability	Impact	Severity	Contingency Plan
Hardware and software compatibility	Low	Medium	Marginal	Purchase compatible hardware
The project will not be completed within the given budget £200 000	Low	High	Marginal	Allow contingency budget
New website not fully functional	Low	High	High	Ensure that the system is fully tested before launch
Software Tester will not be able to apply ISO/IEC 25010:2011 standard	Low	Low	Low	Software Tester to refresh skills in ISO/IEC 25010:2011 standard
Server contractor will not be able deliver and install the system by the required date	Medium	High	High	Provide sufficient notification for delivery and installation date
Network support team of two technicians and IT Help Desk technician support the Software Team Manager, but he is concerned that they might not have the skills required to support the new system requirements	Medium	Medium	Marginal	Sent the network support staff for further training Arrange a separate contract with server contractor to maintain the system until the networking staff confident in the maintenance process
Project not completed within the required date	Low	Low	Low	Monitor project closely, additional staff allocated if required
Securing customer details	High	High	High	Must ensure that all customer data is secure and comply with legal requirements

Deliverables

Suggested answers include:

Item	Components	Description
Online ordering system with an online shopping service	• Orders online interface with business logic • Payment module • Inventory and stock control management • Delivery management • Customer services • Reporting module	• An integrated online ordering system linking payment, updating inventory and stock control that creates a delivery schedule • User friendly reports
Stock control system	• Stock database • Report interface • Supplier link database	• An integrated stock control system that updates the stock database and automated link to supplier for reordering • User friendly reports.

Project quality strategy

Stakeholders

Stakeholders	Responsibility
Managing Director	Responsible for the strategic planning of the organisation
Networking Service Director	Responsible for the network services
Finance Director	Responsible for the organisation finances
Software Team Manager	Responsible for the software team
Quality Manager	Responsible for quality control
Business Manager	Responsible for day to day business processes
Marketing Manager	Responsible for marketing strategy and day to day marketing
Business Analyst	Responsible for identifying the business needs
Server contractor	External; responsible for the consultancy and installation of the new hardware and software

Communication plan

Stakeholder(s)	Frequency	Type	Purpose
Managing Director	Weekly	Weekly expenditure report	Budget update
Finance Director	Weekly	Weekly expenditure report	Budget update
Networking Service Director	Daily	Email	Project progress report
Managing Director	Daily	Email	Project progress report
Finance Director	Daily	Email	Project progress report

Answers to Revision activity 2

(a)

Project stages	09/10/17	09/10/17 Week 1	16/10/17 Week 2	23/10/17 Week 3	30/10/17 Week 4	06/11/17 Week 5	13/11/17 Week 6	20/11/17 Week 7	27/11/17 Week 8	04/12/17 Week 9	11/12/17 Week 10	18/12/17 Week 11	26/12/17 13
Start	■	◇											
Analysis		■	■	◇									
System Design				■	■	◇							
System Development										◇			
Acceptance Testing										■	■	◇	
Installation												■	◇
Launch													■

(b)

Resource list:
Server hardware
Microsoft Windows server
Microsoft SQL server
Web development software
Microsoft Windows Azure
Microsoft Azure cloud storage
Server contractor consultancy and installation
Software Developer monitor
Webpage Developer monitor
Database Administrator monitor
Software Tester laptop

Staffing list:
Project Manager
Business Analyst
Software Team Manager
Database Administrator
Software Developer
Webpage Developer

(c)

Online ordering system and shopping service budget	£200 000		
Resource costs	**Amount**	**Item cost (£)**	**Total cost (£)**
Server hardware	1	30 900	30 900
Microsoft Windows server	1	39 495	39 495
Microsoft SQL server	1	20 356	20 356
Web development software	1	1900	1900
Microsoft Windows Azure	1	4100	4100
Microsoft Azure cloud storage	1	32 000	32 000
		Total Resource costs	**128 751**

	Amount	**Item cost (£)**	**Total cost (£)**
Server contractor consultancy and systems installation	1	39 500	39 500
			39 500

Functional points	**Daily hrs**
Orders online interface with business logic	5
Payment module	2
Inventory and stock control management	3
Delivery management module	3
Total Functional points	**13**

Project team costs	**Day (£)**	**Weeks (£)**	**4 weeks (£)**	**Total 11 weeks (£)**
Project Manager	240	1200	4800	13 200
Business Analyst	228	1140	4560	12 540
Software Team Manager	234	1170	4680	12 870
Software Developer	192	960	3840	10 560
Webpage Developer	192	960	3840	10 560
Database Administrator	192	960	3840	10 560
Software Tester	192	960	3840	10 560
Total Project team costs	**7350**	**29 400**		**80 850**

Additional resource cost per function point	**Hrs**	**FP total**	**Total cost (£)**
Software Team Manager base unit	3	39	1521
Business Analyst	2	26	832
Software Team Manager	2	26	832
Software Developer	2	26	832
Webpage Developer	1	13	416
Total additional resource cost			**4433**

Equipment rental pro-rata cost per week	**Amount**	**Week (£)**	**11 Weeks (£)**
Software Team Manager base unit	1	64	704
Software Developer monitor	1	32	352
Webpage Developer monitor	1	32	352
Database Administrator monitor	1	32	352
Software tester laptop	1	30	330
Total pro-rata cost per week			**2090**

	Total project cost	**255 624**
	Budget	**200 000**
	Project over budget by	**55 624**

Answers to Revision activity 3

Report Details

Date of Checkpoint:	4 December
Period Covered:	System development

Document details

Version	Modifications	Author	Date
3	To account for the 2-week delay for the Database Administrator to update the ordering system and stock control database	Project Manager	4 December
	The Webpage Developer's World Wide Web Consortium (W3C®) course was postponed by a week	Software Team Manager	4 December
	Gantt chart updated as the Webpage Developer was delayed for 1 week on another project	Project Manager	4 December

Document approvals

Name	Role	Signature	Date	Version
Paula Worthy	Managing Director	*Paula Worth*	4 December	3
Sonal Paun	Networking Service Director	*Sonal Paun*	4 December	3
Allan MacInnes	Finance Director	*Allan MacInnes*	4 December	3

Document distribution

Name	Role	Date of Issue	Version
Paula Worthy	Managing Director	4 December	3
Sonal Paun	Networking Service Director	4 December	3
Allan MacInnes	Finance Director	4 December	3
Tom Kotulski	Software Team Manager	4 December	3
Anna Hayton	Quality Manager	4 December	3
George Afua	Business Manager	4 December	3

Products

Product Name	Work Undertaken	Date Complete
Ordering system and stock control database update	Database Administrator updating of the ordering system and stock control database	2 weeks late
Online ordering system/ shopping facility	Payment module Inventory and stock control management Delivery management Stock control database	On time
Webpage interface	Design and development of webpage interface	2 weeks late

Quality Management

During the System Development stage, the Webpage Developer's World Wide Web Consortium (W3C®) course was postponed for a week. However, the Webpage Developer completed his other project and has started to use World Wide Web Consortium (W3C®) standards to create the website. He will review the website when he has completed the course to ensure that the required standards are achieved.

Work Package Tolerance Status

Time:	4 weeks
Cost:	Staff costs approx. £29 400
Quality:	World Wide Web Consortium (W3C®) standards used to create the website

Issues log

Date Raised	Raised By	Description	Action Taken	Date Closed
November	Software Team Manager	Delay in updating the ordering system and stock control database	Database Administrator given more time to work on the update	Ongoing expected end date 15 December
November	Software Team Manager	Webpage Developer's World Wide Web Consortium (W3C®) course was postponed for a week	No action available. Webpage Developer asked to continue with project as specified and review the website when he has completed the course	Ongoing expected end date 29 December

Answers to Revision activity 4

Project closure email

Email	
From	[Your name]
To	Paula Worthy, Managing Director
Subject	Project close: Online ordering system and shopping service

Dear Paula

The project start up was successful. The project was launched on 2 October 2017. However, the project was completed 4 weeks late on 23 January 2018. This was a result of the two week delay in the Database Administrator, to update the ordering system and stock control database, and a further two week delay in developing the webpage.

The original contractor informed the Finance Director on 20 October 2017 that they were unable to install the equipment within the required timeframe. Therefore, it was decided to purchase the new hardware and software from a local contractor, at an additional cost. This did cause a few problems and time as a new contractor had to be sourced. For the next project the tender should include the hardware, software and installation costs.

The Finance Director was happy with the weekly expenditure reports as they allowed him to monitor costs. The daily email also kept him informed of the project progress. This might be a good communication model to use for the next project if the Finance Director is concerned about project budget.

During the system development stage, we had some issues to deal with.
1. The Database Administrator was delayed two weeks in updating the ordering system and stock control database.
2. The Webpage Developer's World Wide Web Consortium (W3C®) course was postponed for a week.
3. The Webpage Developer was also delayed for one week on another project.

The pilot changeover went well and the new online sales website is fully functional. I would recommend this installation method for large systems. This method ensures that each section of the system is tested and operational before moving onto the next stage of the system.

The legal issues of securing customer details were addressed successfully.

The final cost of the project was calculated at £255 624, which was £55 624 over the original budget of £200 000. This was due to the server contractor's additional costs.

The World Wide Web Consortium (W3C®) course caused us some problems. The organisers unexpectedly rescheduled it and also the Webpage Developer.

The server contractor installed the server successfully but it developed a technical fault. The contractor replaced the server free of charge as the contract included a six months' guarantee. I would recommend that at least six months' guarantee is purchased with every hardware resource, in future projects.

The new system reduced overheads by 10 per cent within four months. But the expected return of at least £7500 at the end of three years did not occur. The actual return was £6000. The system increased the number of orders handled from 15 per day to at least 30 per day within the required three months.

The online system has enabled us to carry out a comprehensive review of consumer purchases by products sales analysis. Further analysis is required, but the feedback from customers has been positive. Sports fitness equipment sales have increased by 30 per cent which is higher than the estimated 10 per cent.

The method used to collect customer requirements during the analysis stage was not successful. Only 5 per cent of the questionnaires were returned. The Sales Staff carried out interviews for further Market Research which proved to be both time consuming and also costly and the quality of responses varied by interviewer.

Lessons Learned

More time to be given to the updating of existing systems or allocate more staff to the process.

Source online World Wide Web Consortium (W3C®) courses that can be taken online and at any time.

Investigate other data collection techniques used during the analysis stage.

Provide staff training to all interviews staff to ensure they collect the required information.

Ensure that at least six months' guarantee is purchased with every hardware resource, in future projects.

The project was not completed on time or within budget. Some elements of the system are not fully operational but are ongoing. The majority of the project aims were fulfilled by the project.

Regards

[Your name]

Unit 4: Software Design and Development Project

Answers to Revision task 1

1 BrickBase

2 (i) Conception
(ii) Analysis
(iii) Design
(iv) Implementation
(v) Testing
(vi) Evaluation

3 BrickBase is planning an experimental in-store purchasing system for its trade-only customers as a precursor to investing in a potentially expensive e-commerce version – an online e-commerce website. The aim is to enable customer to self-serve.

4 Remaining CSV data:
"10005","MDF moisture resistant board 2440 x 1220 x 18 mm",27.60,80,20.0,"Lincoln"
"10006","Plywood 2440 x 1220 x 18 mm",31.0,23,20.0,"Bristol"
"10030","Red faced poplar 2440 x 1220 x 18 mm",12.0,44,20.0,"Bristol"
"10031","Red faced poplar 2440 x 1220 x 18 mm",12.0,0,20.0,"Lincoln"
"10045","Coveralls size XL",5.50,45,5.0,"Bristol"
"10046","Condensing boiler safety manual",16.90,10,0.0,"Bristol"

5 Inputs required:
- Customer menu option
- Customer account number
- Product code
- Quantity of product required

6 Processes required:
- Validate product code
- Check a product is in stock
- Add product and quantity to basket
- Calculate cost of product added to basket
- Display menu
- Read product details from the stock file
- Validate customer account
- Calculate total invoice cost of order
- Calculate discount
- Print invoice (basket items and totals)
- Quit when exit option chosen

7 (a) Suggested variables:
- Product code (string)
- Branch Name (string)
- Account number (string)
- Quantity required (integer)
- Sub-total (floating point)
- Discount (floating point)
- Price including VAT (floating point)
- Number of basket items (integer)
- Total (floating point)

(b) Data file which stores stock data for each product.
Suggested examples:
- Product code (string)
- Description (string)
- Price (floating point)
- VAT (floating point)
- Stock level (integer)
- Branch name (string)

8 Outputs required:
- Customer menu options
- Prompt for menu option
- Prompt for customer account
- Prompt for product code
- Customer account details when found
- Product details when found
- Customer account error message when not found
  - Product error message when not found
  - Invoice

9

Test data types	1 Normal	2 Extreme	3 Abnormal
Menu option	1	5	X
Customer account number	DF123	TESTACCOUNTNAME	£$%^&
Product code	10001	10078	ABCDEF
Quantity required	10	1000	ABC

Revision activity 1: Flow chart

Flowchart of in-store purchasing system program (completed)

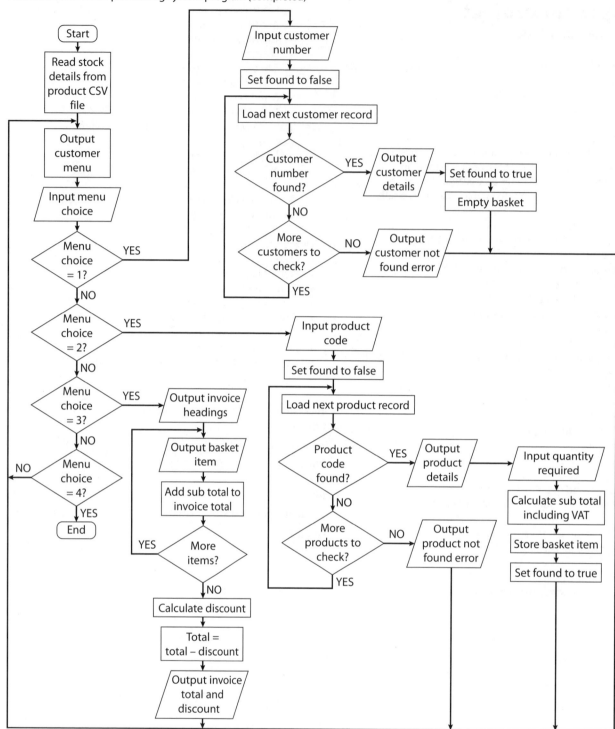

Revision activity 2: Pseudocode

```
STORE customer accounts
READ stock details from file
REPEAT
  OUTPUT customer menu
  INPUT menu choice
  IF menu choice = 1 THEN
    INPUT customer number
    SET found = false
    REPEAT
      READ customer account
      IF customer account = customer number THEN
        OUTPUT customer information
        SET found = true
        SET discount %
      ENDIF
    UNTIL all customer accounts compared
    IF found = false THEN
      OUPUT "Customer not found" error message
    ENDIF
  ELSE
    IF menu choice = 2 THEN
      INPUT product code
      SET found = false
      REPEAT
        READ stock detail
        IF product code = stock detail product code THEN
          OUTPUT stock details
          INPUT quantity required
          Add stock details and quantity to basket
          Subtotal = product code X quantity required
          SET found = true
        ENDIF
      UNTIL all stock details compared
      IF found = false THEN
        OUTPUT "Product code not found" error message
      ENDIF
    ELSE
      IF menu choice = 3 THEN
        OUTPUT Invoice header
        FOR 1 to basket items
          total = total + subtotal
          OUTPUT basket item
        ENDFOR
        total = total — customer discount
        OUTPUT total
        Empty basket
      ENDIF
    ENDIF
  ENDIF
UNTIL menu choice = 4 (exit)
```

Revision activities 3 and 4: Test log

Columns 1–4 of the test log should be completed in Activity 3.
Columns 5 and 6 (shown in grey) should be completed in Activity 4 following testing of your program.

Test number	Purpose of test	Test Data	Expected Result	Actual Result	Comments
| 1 | Menu option 1 chosen | 1 | User asked for account number | ```
- - - - - - - - -
Customer Menu
- - - - - - - - -
1. Login customer
2. Add products to basket
3. Checkout
4. Exit
Please enter your choice (1-4): 1
Please enter your customer number: _
``` | Program works as expected |
| 2 | Invalid (normal) account number input | 1234 | Outputs "Customer not found" error message | ```
Please enter customer number: 1234
Sorry, account '1234' was not found.
- - - - - - - - -
Customer Menu
- - - - - - - - -
1. Login customer
2. Add products to basket
3. Checkout
4. Exit
Please enter your choice (1-4): _
``` | Program works as expected |
| 3 | Valid account number input | DF123 | Customer account information is displayed | ```
Please enter customer number: DF123

Customer Details found:
Account: DF123
Name: A&B Plumbing
Discount: 10%
Address: Withheld
``` | Program works as expected |
| 4 | Menu option 2 chosen | 2 | User asked for product code | ```
Please enter your choice (1-4): 2

Please enter product code: _
``` | Program works as expected |
| 5 | Invalid (normal) product code input | 10101 | "Product code not found" error message | ```
Please enter product code: 10101

Sorry, product code '10101' was not found.
``` | Program works as expected |
| 6 | Valid (normal) product code input | 10001 | Stock details shown and user asked for quantity | ```
Please enter product code: 10001

Product found:
Product code: 10001
Description: MDF board 2440 x 1220 x 18mm
Price ex. VAT: ú14.3
VAT rate: 20%
Please enter quantity required:
``` | Program works as expected |
| 7 | Valid (extreme) quantity input | 999 | Outputs "invalid quantity" error message | ```
Please enter quantity required: 999

- - - - - - - - -
Customer Menu
- - - - - - - - -
1. Login customer
2. Add products to basket
3. Checkout
4. Exit
Please enter your choice (1-4): _
``` | Program does not validate stock levels correctly. |
| 8 | Invalid quantity input | ABC | Outputs "invalid quantity" error message | Screen capture unavailable (program crashes) | Program crashes/ behaves unexpectedly |
| 9 | Valid quantity input | 2 | Item is added to customer basket, menu is redisplayed. | ```
Please enter quantity required: 2

- - - - - - - - -
Customer Menu
- - - - - - - - -
1. Login customer
2. Add products to basket
3. Checkout
4. Exit
Please enter your choice (1-4): _
``` | Program works as expected |
| 10 | Menu option 3 chosen | 3 | Invoice is displayed for the selected customer showing correct item and calculated totals | ```
Please enter your choice (1-4): 3

BRICKBASE INVOICE
- - - - - - - - -
Invoice for A&B Plumbing
Account number: DF123
   Item                                   Description Quantity   Price  Sub-total
   10001                    MDF board 2440 x 1220 x 18 mm    2   14.3     34.32
                                                         Total = ú    30.888
                                                         Saved = ú     3.432
``` | Program works as expected |
| 11 | Menu option 5 chosen (extreme) | 5 | Outputs "Invalid menu option message" | ```
- - - - - - - - -
Customer Menu
- - - - - - - - -
1. Login customer
2. Add products to basket
3. Checkout
4. Exit

Please enter your choice (1-4): 5

- - - - - - - - -
Customer Menu
``` | Program does not display invalid menu option message |

Test number	Purpose of test	Test Data	Expected Result	Actual Result	Comments
12	Menu option X chosen (invalid)	X	Outputs "Invalid menu option message"	Screen capture unavailable (program crashes)	Program crashes/ behaves unexpectedly
13	Menu option 4 chosen	4	Program ends normally	Screen capture unavailable (program ends normally and closes console windows)	Program works as expected

Revision activity 4: Sample C++ solution

(a)

```cpp
#include <iostream>
#include <fstream>
#include <string>
#include <iomanip>

using namespace std;

//function prototypes
void outputCustomerMenu(void);
int readStockDetails(void);

//customer account structure
struct customerAccount {
        string accountNumber;
        string accountName;
        float discountPercentage;
        string shippingAddress;
};

//product structure
struct productDetail {
        string productCode;
        string productDescription;
        float productPrice;
        int inStock;
        float vatPercentage;
        string branch;
};


//basket detail
struct basketDetail {
    int productPosition;
    int quantity;
    float subTotal;
};
```

(b)

```cpp
//constants
const int MAXBASKET = 10;

const int MAXPRODUCTS = 10;


//customer account records
customerAccount Accounts[4] = { { "DF123","A&B Plumbing",10.0f,"Withheld" },
                               { "56789","ConstructCo",7.5f,"Withheld" },
                               { "123765A","Pink Plumbers",5.0f,"Withheld" },
                               { "JONESBUILD","Roofing UK",0.0f,"Withheld" } };
```

```
//products
productDetail Products[MAXPRODUCTS];


//basket items
basketDetail BasketItems[MAXBASKET];
int main() {

    //local declarations

    int menuChoice;                 //menu choice input by user
    string productCode;             //product code input by user
    string customerNumber;          //customer account number input by user
    int quantityRequired;           //quantity of product input by user
    bool found;                     //whether customer or product found
    float subTotal;                 //sub total value of items purchased
    float total;                    //total value of items purchased
    float activeDiscount;           //discount to use
    basketDetail newBasketItem;     //stores a new basket item
    productDetail singleProduct;    //stores a single product
    int basketItemCount;            //count of items in customer basket
    int customerPosition;           //where customer was found in the list
    int productsLoaded;             //how many products loaded from file
    float customerDiscount;         //the calculated customer discount


    //intialisations

    subTotal = 0.0f;
    total = 0.0f;
    activeDiscount = 0.0f;
    basketItemCount = 0;
    customerPosition = 0;
```

(c)

```
    //load the products from file
    productsLoaded = readStockDetails();

do {
    outputCustomerMenu();
    cin >> menuChoice;
    if (menuChoice == 1) {
        cout << "\nPlease enter customer number: ";
        cin.ignore();
        getline(cin, customerNumber);
        found = false;

        for (int counter=0;counter<sizeof(Accounts)/sizeof(*Accounts);counter++){
            if (customerNumber == Accounts[counter].accountNumber) {
                cout << "\n\nCustomer Details found:" << endl;
                cout << "Account: " << Accounts[counter].accountNumber << endl;
                cout << "Name: " << Accounts[counter].accountName << endl;
                cout << "Discount: " << Accounts[counter].discountPercentage << "%" << endl;
                cout << "Address: " << Accounts[counter].shippingAddress << endl;
                found = true;
                activeDiscount = Accounts[counter].discountPercentage;
                basketItemCount = 0;
                customerPosition = counter;
            }
        }
        if (!found) {
```

```
                    cout << "Sorry, account \'"<<customerNumber<<"\' was not found."<<endl;
            }
        }
        else {
            if (menuChoice == 2) {
                cout << "\nPlease enter product code: ";
                cin.ignore();
                getline(cin, productCode);
                found = false;
                for (int counter = 0; counter < productsLoaded; counter++) {
                    if (productCode == Products[counter].productCode) {
                        cout << "\n\nProduct found:" << endl;
                        cout << »Product code: « << Products[counter].productCode << endl;
                        cout << »Description: « << Products[counter].productDescription << endl;
                        cout << »Price ex. VAT: £" << Products[counter].productPrice << endl;
                        cout << "Vat Rate: "<< Products[counter].vatPercentage << "%" << endl;
                        cout << "Branch: " << Products[counter].branch << endl;
                        cout << "Please enter quantity required: ";
                        cin >> quantityRequired;
                        subTotal = quantityRequired * Products[found].productPrice * <…>
                        (1 + Products[found].vatPercentage / 100);
                        newBasketItem.productPosition = counter;
                        newBasketItem.quantity = quantityRequired;
                        newBasketItem.subTotal = subTotal;
                        BasketItems[basketItemCount++] = newBasketItem;
                        found = true;
                    }
                }
                if (!found) {
                    cout << "\n\nSorry, product code \'" << productCode << "\' was not found." << endl;
                }
            }
```

(d)

```
        else {
            if (menuChoice == 3) {
                cout << "\n\n\nBRICKBASE INVOICE" << endl;
                cout << "-----------------" << endl;
                cout << "\nInvoice for" << Accounts[customerPosition].accountName << endl;
                cout << "Account number : " << Accounts[customerPosition].accountNumber << endl;
                cout << endl << setw(8) << "Item" << setw(50) << "Description" << setw(10);
                cout << "Quantity" << setw(8) << "Price" << setw(10) << "Sub-total" << endl;
                for (int counter = 0; counter < basketItemCount; counter++) {
                    total = total + BasketItems[counter].subTotal;
                    singleProduct = Products[BasketItems[counter].productPosition];
                    cout << setw(8) << singleProduct.productCode;
                    cout << setw(50) << singleProduct.productDescription;
                    cout << setw(10) << BasketItems[counter].quantity;
                    cout << setw(8) << singleProduct.productPrice;
                    cout << setw(10) << BasketItems[counter].subTotal << endl;
                }
                customerDiscount= (total/100*Accounts[customerPosition].discountPercentage);
                total = total - customerDiscount;
                cout << endl << setw(76) << "Total = £" << setw(10) << total << endl;
                cout << setw(76) << "Saved = £" << setw(10) << customerDiscount << endl;
            }
        }
    }

} while (menuChoice!= 4);
```

```
        return 0;
}
/*
 * function to display customer menu options
 *
 */
void outputCustomerMenu(void) {
        cout << "\n\n-------------" << endl;
        cout << "Customer Menu" << endl;
        cout << "-------------" << endl;
        cout << "1. Login customer" << endl;
        cout << "2. Add products to basket" << endl;
        cout << "3. Checkout" << endl;
        cout << "4. Exit" << endl;
        cout << "\nPlease enter your choice (1-4): ";
}
```

(e)

```
/*
 * function to read stock details from CSV file and
 * store in as an array of products
 *
 * returns the number of products read from CSV file.
 */
int readStockDetails(void) {
        ifstream productFile;
        int productLine;
        string tempString;

        productLine = 0;
        productFile.open("products.csv");
        while (!productFile.eof()) {
            //get product code and remove quotes
            getline(productFile, Products[productLine].productCode, ',');
            Products[productLine].productCode.erase(0,1);
            Products[productLine].productCode.erase(Products[productLine]. productCode.size()-1);

            //get product description and remove quotes
            getline(productFile, Products[productLine].productDescription, ',');
            Products[productLine].productDescription.erase(0, 1);

            Products[productLine].productDescription.erase(Products[productLine].productDescription.
            size() -  1);

            //get product price and convert to float
            getline(productFile, tempString, ',');
            Products[productLine].productPrice = ::atof(tempString.c_str());

            //get in stock and convert to float
            getline(productFile, tempString, ',');
            Products[productLine].inStock = ::atof(tempString.c_str());

            //get VAT rate and convert to float
            getline(productFile, tempString, ',');
            Products[productLine].vatPercentage = ::atof(tempString.c_str());

            //get branch and remove quotes
            getline(productFile, Products[productLine].branch,'\n');
            Products[productLine].branch.erase(0, 1);
            Products[productLine].branch.erase(Products[productLine].branch.size() - 1);
            //next product
            productLine++;
```

```
        }
        productFile.close();
        return --productLine;
}
```

Revision activity 4: Sample Python solution

(a)

```python
import csv

#function to read stock details from CSV file
def readStockDetails():
  productFile = open('products.csv','r')
  reader = csv.reader(productFile)
  for eachProduct in reader:
     Products.append(eachProduct)
  productFile.close()

#function to display customer menu options
def outputCustomerMenu():
  print('-------------')
  print('Customer Menu')
  print('-------------')
  print('1. Login customer')
  print('2. Add products to basket')
  print('3. Checkout')
  print('4. Exit')
  print('Please enter your choice (1-4):')


#customer account record
Accounts = {1: {'accountNumber': 'DF123', 'accountName': 'A&B Plumbing', 'discountPercentage' :10.0,
<...>
'shippingAddress': 'Withheld'},
          2: {'accountNumber': '56789', 'accountName': 'ConstructCo', 'discountPercentage' :7.5,  <...>
'shippingAddress': 'Withheld'},
          3: {'accountNumber': '123765A', 'accountName': 'Pink Plumbers', 'discountPercentage' :5.0,
<...>
'shippingAddress': 'Withheld'},
          4: {'accountNumber': 'JONESBUILD', 'accountName': 'Roofing UK', 'discountPercentage' :0.0,
<...>
'shippingAddress': 'Withheld'}}

#products
Products = []

#basket items
BasketItems = [[] for _ in range(10)]

newBasketItem = [0,0,0]
singleProduct = []

#intitialisations
activeDiscount = 0
basketItemCount = 0
customerPosition = 0
quantityRequired = 0
total = 0

#load the products from file
readStockDetails()

while True:
    outputCustomerMenu()
```

```
    menuChoice = int(input())
    found = False

    if (menuChoice == 1):
      customerNumber = input('Please enter customer number: ')
      for eachAccount, value in Accounts.items():
        if customerNumber == value['accountNumber']:
          print('Customer Details found:')
          print('Account: ', value['accountNumber'])
          print('Account: ', value['discountPercentage'],'%')
          print('Account: ', value['shippingAddress'])
          found = True;
          activeDiscount = value['discountPercentage']
          basketItemCount = 0
          total = 0
```

(b)

```
          customerPosition = eachAccount
        if (not found):
          print('Sorry, account, "', customerNumber, '" was not found.')
    else:
      if (menuChoice == 2):
        productCode = input('Please enter product code: ')
        found = False
        for index, eachProduct in enumerate(Products):
          if productCode == eachProduct[0]:
            print('Product found:')
            print('Product code: ', eachProduct[0])
            print('Description: ', eachProduct[1])
            print('Price ex. VAT: £', eachProduct[2])
            print('Vat Rate: ', eachProduct[4],'%')
            print('Branch: ', eachProduct[5])

            quantityRequired = int(input('Please enter quantity required: '))
            subTotal = quantityRequired * float(eachProduct[2]) * (1+float(eachProduct[4])/100)
            newBasketItem = [index, quantityRequired, subTotal]
            BasketItems[basketItemCount] = newBasketItem
            basketItemCount = basketItemCount + 1
            found = True;

        if (not found):
          print('Sorry, product code, "', productCode, '" was not found.')

      else:
        if (menuChoice == 3):
          print ('BRICKBASE INVOICE')
          print ('----------------')
          print ('Invoice for ', Accounts[customerPosition]['accountName'])
          print ('Account number : ', Accounts[customerPosition]['accountNumber'])
          print ('{:>8}'.format('Item'),'{:>50}'.format('Description'),end='')
          print ('{:>10}'.format('Quantity'),'{:>8}'.format('Price'),end='')
          print ('{:>10}'.format('Sub-total'))
          for counter in range (0, basketItemCount):
            total = total + BasketItems[counter][2]
            singleProduct = Products[BasketItems[counter][0]]
            print('{:>8}'.format(singleProduct[0]),end='')
            print('{:>50}'.format(singleProduct[1]),end='')
            print('{:>10}'.format(BasketItems[counter][1]),end='')
            print('{:>8}'.format(singleProduct[2]),end='')
            print('{:>10}'.format(BasketItems[counter][2]))
          customerDiscount = (total /100 * Accounts[customerPosition]['discountPercentage'])
```

```
      total = total - customerDiscount
      print ('{:>76}'.format('Total = £'), '{:>10}'.format(total))
      print ('{:>76}'.format('Saved = £'), '{:>10}'.format(customerDiscount))

    else:
      if (menuChoice == 4):
        break;
```

Revision activity 5: Review and evaluation

Software Evaluation:

Evaluation of the design

The design has covered the basic specification as described by the client. The flow chart uses the BCS symbols correctly and presents a workable solution. The pseudocode is generally sound and covers the majority of the inputs, outputs and processes using recognised key words.

One aspect of the design has been missed. This is the validation which prevents the customer from ordering a quantity of product which is greater than the product's current stock level. Neither is there any attempt to reduce the available stock level (in memory or in file) once the products have been purchased (this is outside the project's scope for now).

Evaluation of the software testing

The test plan has identified the major inputs for the solution and attempts have been made to test a range of data. However, testing could be improved by using a greater range of data, particularly deliberately invalid/erroneous values (e.g. inputting strings for numeric inputs) which could cause the program to crash or perform unexpectedly. In addition, there is no evidence of testing multiple customer logins to check that the basket is correctly emptied. Testing should also confirm that calculations have been performed correctly (for an order's sub-totals and totals by showing the actual working involved), especially for multiple order items.

Evaluation of the software

The coding has been written using a range of program language components and, generally, has meaningful identifier names and uses indentation consistently to highlight the structure and logic of the solution. The products are successfully read from a CSV data file using a separate function. During testing the program worked reliably and produced accurate results in an efficient manner. Data types and structures are well chosen and appropriately mirror the real-world data they represent.

Functions have been created to read the products from the CSV product file and display the customer menu options, however the overall readability could be improved by splitting the separate menu options into different functions.

The solution is incomplete and does not fully meet the needs of the client. In particular, it is possible to order quantities of a product which are not actually available as no check is made to validate this quantity. In addition, there are minor formatting issues, particularly when displaying currency where no attempt has been made to format these sums to two decimal places.

Answers to Revision task 2
Revision activity 1: Flow chart

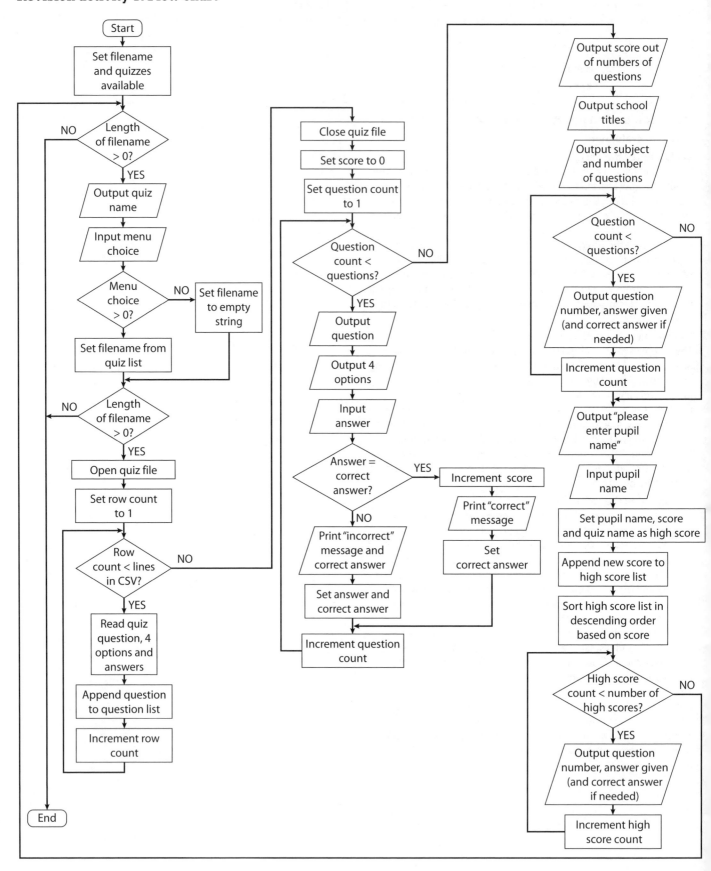

Revision activity 2: Pseudocode

```
SET Filename = 'NOFILE'
SET Quizzes available = 'Science','Mathematics','Geography'
WHILE length of filename > 0
  OUTPUT "Select Quiz"
  FOR 1 to Quizzes
    OUTPUT menu option and quiz title
  ENDFOR
  OUTPUT "Enter your choice or 0 to quit"
  INPUT choice
  IF choice > 0 THEN
    SELECT quiz filename from list of quizzes available
  ELSE
    Filename = ''
  ENDIF
  IF length of filename > 0 THEN
    OPEN quiz file (CSV)
    FOR 1 to number of rows in quiz file (CSV)
      READ quiz question, 4 options and correct answer
      APPEND question to questions
    ENDFOR
    CLOSE quiz file (CSV)
    SET score = 0
    FOR 1 to number of questions
      OUTPUT question
      OUTPUT 4 options
      INPUT answer
      IF answer = correct answer THEN
        score = score + 1
        PRINT "Correct!" message
        SET correct answer
      ELSE
        PRINT "Incorrect" message and the correct answer
        SET answer and correct answer
      ENDIF
    ENDFOR
    OUTPUT score "out of " number of questions
    OUTPUT "Manor Road Primary School"
    OUTPUT "Quiz"
    OUTPUT Subject and number of questions
    FOR 1 to answers
      OUTPUT Question number, answer given (and correct answer if needed)
    ENDFOR
    OUTPUT "Please enter pupil name"
    INPUT pupil name
    SET pupil name, score and quiz name as high score
    APPEND new high score to high score list
    SORT high score list in descending order based on score
    OUTPUT "High Score table "
    FOR 1 to high score entries
      OUTPUT high score entry (name, score and quiz name)
    ENDFOR
  ENDIF
ENDWHILE
```

Revision activities 3 and 4: Test log

Columns 1–4 of the test log should be completed in Activity 3.
Columns 5 and 6 (shown in grey) should be completed in Activity 4 following testing of your program.

Test number	Purpose of test	Test Data	Expected Result	Actual Result	Comments
1	Test exit from menu	0	Program ends normally	``` Select Quiz ---------- 1 : Science 2 : Mathematics 3 : Geography Enter your choice (0 to quit): 0 >>> ```	Works as expected
2	Choose science quiz questions	1	Program loads science questions from correct CSV file and asks first question.	``` Select Quiz ---------- 1 : Science 2 : Mathematics 3 : Geography Enter your choice (0 to quit): 1 Loading Science questions. Question 1 Which word is used to describe something that is dog-like? A. Feline B. Piscine C. Canine D. Porcine Enter A, B, C or D: ```	Works as expected
3	Test question 1 answer (normal)	C	Question is answered correctly, score increases and question 2 is shown	``` Enter A, B, C or D: C Correct! Question 2 Which is the largest planet in our solar system? A. Jupiter B. Saturn C. Mars D. Mercury Enter A, B, C or D: ```	Works as expected
4	Test question 2 answer (normal)	B	Question is answered incorrectly, score doesn't increase, question 3 is shown	``` Enter A, B, C or D: B Incorrect, the correct answer was: A Question 3 What is the pH level of water? A. 7 B. 4 C. 1 D. 9 Enter A, B, C or D: ```	Works as expected
5	Test question 3 answer	B	Question is answered incorrectly, score doesn't increase, question 4 is shown	``` Enter A, B, C or D: A Incorrect, the correct answer was: B Question 4 What is a tomato? A. Vegetable B. Fruit C. Nut D. Seed Enter A, B, C or D: ```	Works as expected
6	Test question 4 answer	D	Question is answered incorrectly, score doesn't increase, question 5 is shown.	``` Enter A, B, C or D: D Incorrect, the correct answer was: A Question 5 What is the young of a squirrel called? A. Kit B. Calf C. Gosling D. Infant Enter A, B, C or D: ```	Works as expected

Test number	Purpose of test	Test Data	Expected Result	Actual Result	Comments
7	Test question 5 answer (extreme)	E	Program displays error message (invalid option) because E isn't a valid input!	```Enter A, B, C or D: E
Incorrect, the correct answer was: A
You scored 1 out of 5
Manor Road Primary School
Quiz
Subject Science (5 questions available)
Question 1 : Correct (C)
Question 2 : Incorrect, the correct answer
was B
Question 3 : Incorrect, the correct answer
was A
Question 4 : Incorrect, the correct answer
was A
Question 5 : Incorrect, the correct answer
was B
Please enter your name:```	Doesn't work as expected – Breakdown of how each question is answered is shown. Pupil is asked for their name.
8	Test pupil name input	Jane	High score table is displayed showing Jane's score and Quiz select menu is shown again.	```Please enter your name: Jane
High score table
1 Jane scored 1 on Science
Select Quiz
----
1 : Science
2 : Mathematics
3 : Geography
Enter your choice (0 to quit):```	Works as expected

Sample CSV, e.g. Science.csv

```
"Which word is used to describe something that is dog-like?", "Feline", "Piscine", "Canine", "Porcine","C"
"Which is the largest planet in our solar system?","Jupiter","Saturn","Mars","Mercury","A"
"What is the pH level of water?","7","4","1","9","A"
"What is a tomato?","Vegetable","Fruit","Nut","Seed","B"
"What is the young of a squirrel called?","Kit","Calf","Gosling","Infant","A"
```

Note. Three suitably formatted csv files would be required, for example, Science.csv, Geography.csv and Mathematics.csv

These should be created using a text editor (not a word processor) and should not have any additional blank lines or unexpected characters.

Revision activity 4: Python Program code

```python
import csv

#function to select from available quizzes
def selectQuiz():
   print ('Select Quiz')
   print ('-----------')
   for index, subject in enumerate(quizSubjects):
      print (index+1,' : ', subject)
   choice = int(input('Enter your choice (0 to quit): '))
   if (choice > 0):
      filename = quizSubjects[choice-1]
   else:
      filename=''

   return filename


#function to load a quiz from a CSV file
def loadQuiz(filename):
  print('Loading',filename,'questions.')
  quizFile = open('%s.csv' % filename, 'r')
  reader = csv.reader(quizFile)
  for eachQuestion in reader:
     questions.append(eachQuestion)
  quizFile.close()
  return


#function to show the selected quiz
def showQuiz(score):
  for index, eachQuestion in enumerate(questions):
     print ('Question ',index+1)
     print (eachQuestion[0])
```

```python
      print ('A. ',eachQuestion[1])
      print ('B. ',eachQuestion[2])
      print ('C. ',eachQuestion[3])
      print ('D. ',eachQuestion[4])
      answer = input('Enter A, B, C or D: ')
      if answer == eachQuestion[5]:
         score = score + 1
         print('Correct!')
         answers.append('Correct (' + answer + ')')
      else:
         print('Incorrect, the correct answer was: ',end='')
         print(eachQuestion[5])
         answers.append('Incorrect, the correct answer was: ' + eachQuestion[5])

   print('You scored ', score,' out of ', len(questions))
   return score

def highScoreTable(score):
   pupilName = input ("Please enter your name:")
   highscoreEntry = [score, pupilName, filename]
   #append to high score table
   highscore.append(highscoreEntry)
   #sort on score, descending order
   highscore.sort(key=lambda x: x[0], reverse=True)
   #print the high score table
   print ('High score table')
   for index, highscoreEntry in enumerate(highscore):
      print(index+1, highscoreEntry[1],' scored ',end='')
      print(highscoreEntry[0],' on ', highscoreEntry [2])

   return

#show breakdown of questions
def showScore(filename):
   print ('Manor Road Primary School')
   print ('Quiz')
   print('Subject ',filename, '(', len(questions) ,' questions available)')
   for index, answer in enumerate(answers):
      print ('Question ',index+1,': ',answer)
   return

#declarations and initialisation
quizSubjects = ['Science','Mathematics','Geography']
questions = []
answers = []
highscoreEntry = []
highscore = []
score = 0
choice = 1
pupilName= ''
filename = 'nofile'

#main program loops until exit (0) chosen
while (len(filename) > 0):
   #reset score, loaded questions and answers each time
   score = 0
   questions = []
   answers = []
   filename = selectQuiz()
   if len(filename) > 0:
      loadQuiz(filename)
      score = showQuiz(score)
      showScore(filename)
      highScoreTable(score)
```

Revision activity 4 C++ Program code

```cpp
// SchoolQuiz.cpp
// Note.  This version uses STL library sort function and a comparator

#include "stdafx.h"
#include <iostream>
#include <fstream>
#include <string>
#include <algorithm>

using namespace std;

struct ahighscoreEntry;

//function prototypes
string selectQuiz(void);
int loadQuiz(string);
int showQuiz(int);
void highScoreTable(int, string);
void showScore(int, int, string);
bool comparator(ahighscoreEntry const &, ahighscoreEntry const &);

//declarations and initialisation

struct ahighscoreEntry {
  string pupilName;
  int score;
  string filename;
};

struct aQuestion {
  string questionText;
  string answerA;
  string answerB;
  string answerC;
  string answerD;
  string correctAnswer;
};
const int SUBJECTCOUNT = 3;
const int MAXQUESTIONS = 20;
const int MAXHIGHSCORECOUNT = 20;

string quizSubjects[SUBJECTCOUNT] = { "Science", "Mathematics", "Geography" };
aQuestion questions[MAXQUESTIONS];
string answers[MAXQUESTIONS];
ahighscoreEntry highscore[MAXHIGHSCORECOUNT];
int highscoreCount = 0;

int main()
{
  string filename;
  int questionCount;
  int score;
  int answersCount;

  filename = "noname";
  while (filename.length() > 0) {

    //reset score, loaded questions and answers each time
    score = 0;
    answersCount = 0;

    filename = selectQuiz();
    if (filename.length() > 0) {
```

175

```cpp
      questionCount = loadQuiz(filename);
      score = showQuiz(questionCount);
      showScore(score, questionCount, filename);
      highScoreTable(score, filename);
    }
  }
  return 0;
}

//function to select from available quizzes
string selectQuiz(void) {
  string filename;
  int index;
  int choice;

  cout << "Select Quiz" << endl;
  cout << "-----------" << endl;
  for (index = 0; index < SUBJECTCOUNT; index++) {
    cout << index + 1 << " : " << quizSubjects[index] << endl;
  }
  cout << "Enter your choice (0 to quit): ";
  cin >> choice;
  if (choice > 0) {
    filename = quizSubjects[choice - 1];
  }
  else {
    filename = "";
  }
  return filename;
}
//function to load a quiz from a CSV file
int loadQuiz(string filename) {
  ifstream quizFile;
  int quizQuestionCount;

  cout << "Loading " << filename << " questions." << endl;
  quizQuestionCount = 0;
  quizFile.open(filename + ".csv");

  while (!quizFile.eof()) {
    //get question text and remove quotes
    getline(quizFile, questions[quizQuestionCount].questionText, ',');
    questions[quizQuestionCount].questionText.erase(0, 1);
    questions[quizQuestionCount].questionText.erase(questions[quizQuestionCount].questionText.size()-1);

    //get answer A and remove quotes
    getline(quizFile, questions[quizQuestionCount].answerA, ',');
    questions[quizQuestionCount].answerA.erase(0, 1);
    questions[quizQuestionCount].answerA.erase(questions[quizQuestionCount].answerA.size() - 1);

    //get answer B and remove quotes
    getline(quizFile, questions[quizQuestionCount].answerB, ',');
    questions[quizQuestionCount].answerB.erase(0, 1);
    questions[quizQuestionCount].answerB.erase(questions[quizQuestionCount].answerB.size() - 1);

    //get answer C and remove quotes
    getline(quizFile, questions[quizQuestionCount].answerC, ',');
    questions[quizQuestionCount].answerC.erase(0, 1);
    questions[quizQuestionCount].answerC.erase(questions[quizQuestionCount].answerC.size() - 1);

    //get answer D and remove quotes
    getline(quizFile, questions[quizQuestionCount].answerD, ',');
    questions[quizQuestionCount].answerD.erase(0, 1);
    questions[quizQuestionCount].answerD.erase(questions[quizQuestionCount].answerD.size() - 1);
```

```
      //get correct answer and remove quotes
      getline(quizFile, questions[quizQuestionCount].correctAnswer, '\n');
      questions[quizQuestionCount].correctAnswer.erase(0, 1);
      questions[quizQuestionCount].correctAnswer.erase(questions[quizQuestionCount]
      .correctAnswer.size()-1);

      quizQuestionCount++;
   }
   return quizQuestionCount;
}

//function to show the selected quiz
int showQuiz(int questionCount) {
   int index;
   string singleAnswer;
   string answer;

   int score = 0;
   for (index = 0; index < questionCount; index++) {
      cout << «Question « << index + 1 << endl;
      cout << questions[index].questionText << endl;
      cout << «A. « << questions[index].answerA << endl;
      cout << «B. « << questions[index].answerB << endl;
      cout << «C. « << questions[index].answerC << endl;
      cout << «D. « << questions[index].answerD << endl;
      cout << "Enter A, B, C or D: " << endl;
      cin >> answer;
      if (answer == questions[index].correctAnswer) {
         score++;
         cout << "Correct!" << endl;
         singleAnswer = "Correct (" + answer + ')';
         answers[index] = singleAnswer;
      }

      else {
         cout << "Incorrect, the correct answer was: ";
         cout << questions[index].correctAnswer << endl;
         singleAnswer = "Incorrect, the correct answer was: " + questions[index].correctAnswer;
         answers[index] = singleAnswer;
      }
   }
   cout << "You scored " << score << " out of " << questionCount << endl;
   return score;
}

void highScoreTable(int score, string filename) {
   string pupilName;
   ahighscoreEntry highscoreEntry;
   int index;

   cout << "Please enter your name:";
   cin >> pupilName;

   highscoreEntry.score = score;
   highscoreEntry.pupilName = pupilName;
   highscoreEntry.filename = filename;

   //append to high score table
   highscore[highscoreCount] = highscoreEntry;
   highscoreCount++;

   //sort on score, descending order
   //order highscore using standard library sort
```

```
    sort(highscore, highscore + highscoreCount, &comparator);

    //print the high score table
    cout << "High score table" << endl;

    for (index = 0; index < highscoreCount; index++) {
      cout << index + 1 << ' ' << highscore[index].pupilName << " scored ";
      cout << highscore[index].score << " on ";
      cout << highscore[index].filename << endl;
    }
  }


//show breakdown of questions
void showScore(int score, int questionCount, string filename) {
  int index;

  cout << "Manor Road Primary School" << endl;
  cout << «Quiz» << endl;
  cout << «Subject « << filename << « (« << questionCount << « questions available)» << endl;
  for (index = 0; index < questionCount; index++) {
    cout << "Question " << index + 1 << ": " << answers[index] << endl;
  }
}


//customer comparator for standard sort routine
bool comparator(ahighscoreEntry const &firstScore, ahighscoreEntry const &secondScore) {
  return firstScore.score > secondScore.score;
}
```

Revision activity 5: Review and evaluation
Exemplar answer uses Python.

Evaluation of the design
The design has generally met the requirements of the client. Questions, options and correct answers have been stored in a CSV file and these are read into arrays. A menu system is used to display the available subjects. These are preset for now rather than searching a folder for available subject files (this could be improved). The flow chart uses standard symbols and the pseudocode is written in good detail (assisting its conversion to a target programming language) with indentation highlighting the structure of the code. The design doesn't explain how the sorting of the learner's score will be performed to create a high-score table. Some error handling is also missing, for example, there is nothing to prevent a learner from entering an answer which isn't A, B, C or D.

Evaluation of the software testing
The test plan is quite limited and only includes one test run through the program (using the science sample questions provided). Extreme data has been used to test error handling and it has helped to identify the factor that invalid options can be entered (they will assumed to be incorrect). Normal data includes test of various menu options and answers and these appear to work well. The expected answers have been matched to screen captures generated by a Python 3.5 version of the solution. Although actual and expected differences have been noted, I haven't explained how to improve this in the program code. To improve testing, I would test other question sets and entering more extreme data, for example, numbers and words instead of single letters (A, B, C, D etc).

Evaluation of the software
The program code has been written in a modular fashion using a number of functions to break the solution into definable parts, for example, showing the menu, showing the questions etc. Various library functions are used to load the CSV file and sort the scores in the high-score table. A variety of standard selection and loop statements have been used to perform the basic logic of the program. Screen output is very basic and there has been no attempt to produce colour or graphics on screen; this may mean it becomes very boring to use. In addition, actual testing shows that a few blank lines and perhaps better alignment could be used to improve the display. The code is commented in key areas and indentation is used to highlight the structure of the program, generally following the pseudocode that was produced earlier. Identifier names (variables, constants and functions) are meaningful and easy to understand. Good use has been made of Python features including list data structures and their useful methods (such as append). Python's CSV library makes it very easy to import this type of file. Although a few improvements are possible the program is fast, responsive and generally reliable to use.

Notes

Notes